At Issue

Are Government Bailouts Effective?

Other Books in the At Issue Series:

At Issue

| Are Government
| Bailouts Effective?

Louise I. Gerdes, Book Editor

GREENHAVEN PRESS
A part of Gale, Cengage Learning

GALE
CENGAGE Learning·

Detroit • New York • San Francisco • New Haven, Conn • Waterville, Maine • London

GALE
CENGAGE Learning·

Elizabeth Des Chenes, *Director, Publishing Solutions*

© 2013 Greenhaven Press, a part of Gale, Cengage Learning.

Gale and Greenhaven Press are registered trademarks used herein under license.

For more information, contact:
Greenhaven Press
27500 Drake Rd.
Farmington Hills, MI 48331-3535
Or you can visit our Internet site at www.gale.cengage.com

Articles in Greenhaven Press anthologies are often edited for length to meet page requirements. In addition, original titles of these works are changed to clearly present the main thesis and to explicitly indicate the author's opinion. Every effort is made to ensure that Greenhaven Press accurately reflects the original intent of the authors. Every effort has been made to trace the owners of copyrighted material.

LIBRARY OF CONGRESS CATALOGING-IN-PUBLICATION DATA

Are government bailouts effective? / Louise I. Gerdes, book editor.
p. cm. -- (At issue)
Includes bibliographical references and index.
ISBN 978-0-7377-6179-5 (hbk.) -- ISBN 978-0-7377-6180-1 (pbk.)
1. Financial crises--Government policy--United States. 2. Bailouts (Government policy)--United States. 3. Intervention (Federal government)--United States. 4. Bankruptcy--Prevention--Government policy--United States. 5. United States--Economic conditions--2009- I. Gerdes, Louise I., 1953-
HB3743.A72 2012
338.973'02--dc23
                                                                    2012024912

Printed in the United States of America
1 2 3 4 5 6 7 16 15 14 13 12

Contents

Introduction

President George W. Bush addressed the nation on September 24, 2008, as the US financial crisis intensified in a cascade of events. The calamity began with the seizure by the federal government of struggling home mortgage giants Fannie Mae and Freddie Mac and was followed by the collapse of the investment banking giant Lehman Brothers in the largest bankruptcy in American history. In response, Bush warned on national television that without a rescue plan, "America could slip into a financial panic." He warned of further business failures, job loss, and home foreclosures. Although Congress had been bitterly divided in recent years, in September and October 2008 lawmakers were unified in their anger and frustration. For years the nation's financial analysts and Wall Street experts ensured them that an unregulated marketplace would thrive and that economic growth and prosperity would continue. Despite these promises, investment banks failed, the real estate market collapsed, and homeowners were unable to pay their mortgages. "We were told that markets knew best, and that we were entering a new world of global growth and prosperity,"[1] claims Senator Charles E. Schumer, chairman of the Joint Economic Committee. "We now have to pay for the greed and recklessness of those who should have known better."[2] American lawmakers faced a dilemma: to prevent an economic meltdown, they could save Wall Street, but by doing so they would risk the ire of their Main Street constituents and the loss of their congressional seats.

Despite these risks, on October 3, 2008, lawmakers overcame their differences and authorized the US Treasury to

---

1. Quoted in David Stout, "Fed Chief Calls Delay a Threat to the Economy," *New York Times*, September 25, 2008.
2. *Ibid.*

spend up to $700 billion to purchase "toxic"[3] mortgage-backed securities from Wall Street and invest in the nation's banks to unlock a credit freeze that threatened to stifle economic growth. In addition, the government loaned $29 billion to investment bank JP Morgan Chase to acquire the struggling Bear Stearns, had invested $200 billion before it seized Fannie Mae and Freddie Mac, and after providing it with $12 billion, took over the insurance giant American International Group. In the end, the bailout package approached $1 trillion, far exceeding any other bailout in US history. While anger over the bailout was and continues to be widespread, analysts disagree on the root causes of the financial crisis and thus whether the bailout has, in fact, worked. Indeed, the debates at the time of the bailout over what factors led to the financial crisis reflect the complexity of the bailout debate today.

Some believed in 2008 that the primary reason for the financial crisis was a loss of confidence in financial institutions. Because financial institutions worldwide borrowed to invest in mortgages, when the real estate market collapsed and mortgage defaults rose, the risk of insolvency discouraged investors and worried creditors. This created a lack of confidence, which discouraged lending, which in turn froze consumer and business credit. In the minds of analysts who believed lost confidence was the cause, the bailout was necessary to restore that confidence. "The rescue plan is a smart thing,"[4] claimed Claremont McKenna College economics professor Gregory Hess in 2008. "You have to give credit markets every chance to create confidence and unwind the systemic uncertainty in the market. What monetary policy does and what finance does is that literally we're just trading pieces of paper,"[5] Hess maintained.

---

3. The word "toxic" is a term that has been applied to financial instruments that cannot be identified as an asset or a liability and their value has fallen significantly and may fall further, especially when the market for them has frozen.
4. As quoted in Thomas J. Billitteri, "Financial Bailout," *CQ Researcher*, October 24, 2008.
5. *Ibid.*

"And until the Fed and the Treasury can create confidence and those pieces of paper are meaningful and trustworthy, we're not going to get out of this credit collapse."[6] Other economic analysts disagreed. They argued that saving homeowners would do more to restore confidence than saving banks. University of Missouri-Kansas City economics professor Randall Wray countered, "Several hundred billion into the hands of consumers will do a lot more than $700 billion in the hands of Wall Street."[7]

Indeed, many analysts claimed at the time of the bailout that the cause of the crisis was the collapse of the real estate market. They maintained that record-low interest rates early in the decade stimulated lending and created a housing bubble. Some lenders believed that even borrowers with bad credit or without documented income could refinance based on rising home values. These lending speculators were ultimately wrong. Home prices fell, and with many homeowners owing more than their homes were worth, mortgage defaults and foreclosures increased. This in turn hurt lenders who borrowed heavily to purchase mortgage-backed securities. Thus, for those who believed the collapse of the housing bubble was the cause of the financial crisis, the bailout would not work. In their view it did nothing to stop "the fundamental cause of the crises: the downward spiral of house prices that devastates household wealth and destroys the capital of financial institutions that hold mortgage backed securities,"[8] wrote Harvard economics professor Martin Feldstein. He argued in 2008 that helping struggling homeowners with a limited number of federal mortgage-replacement loans would help break the downward plunge of house prices.

Even among bailout critics who at the time believed that banks would eventually start lending more freely, some were

6. *Ibid.*
7. *Ibid.*
8. Martin Feldstein, "The Problem Is Still Falling House Prices," *Wall Street Journal*, October 4, 2008.

concerned that the bailout would do nothing to stop banks from returning to the irresponsible practices that led to the crisis. Auburn University economics professor Robert Ekelund feared that banks would have the attitude that "if they make mistakes, they'll be bailed out."[9] These analysts believed then and now that a failed regulatory system led to the financial crises. Without reform, they argued, the rescue plan would fail to prevent future bailouts. According to John Bohn, a former banker, "Wall Street is driven by two emotions, fear and greed"[10] Thus, Bohn adds, "When the fear of excessive risk goes away, greed does what it is expected to do. That is what happened. The whole mess is a monumental failure of regulation."[11]

Some of those who in 2008 blamed failed regulation also believed that the regulatory system had not kept up with changes in the financial system. They maintained that the system was designed for a time when commercial banks supported the financial system, but today, the financial system is more complex. Indeed, investment banks, insurance companies, and hedge funds have become as important as commercial banks. However, they are not subject to the same regulatory oversight. Professor Hess at the time of the bailout asserted, "We did not keep up with the pace of financial innovation. We need to regulate as new products are being developed, not after we've found out which ones don't work."[12] During the 2008-bailout debates, Roger Leeds, the director of Johns Hopkins University's Center for International Business and Public Policy, claimed that the regulatory framework is "egregiously fragmented. There are too many regulatory institutions, and coordination among them is inadequate—they don't talk to each other effectively."[13] Some, however, opposed

9. As quoted in Billitteri, *op. cit.*
10. *Ibid.*
11. *Ibid.*
12. *Ibid.*
13. *Ibid.*

significant regulatory reform, arguing that the bailout would fail not because of a lack of regulation but because risky behavior goes unpunished—often called a "moral hazard." According to Norman Ornstein, of the free market think tank the American Enterprise Institute, "The most important thing when restoring the long-term health of the financial system is to recreate the balance between risk and reward, and between benefits for exemplary performance and punishment for malfeasance or nonfeasance."[14]

The debate over how best to regulate the financial system, begun in 2008, continues. Amid this debate, in July 2010, President Barack Obama signed into law a plan to better regulate the financial system. By that time much of the bailout money had been repaid. Thus, some analysts, such as Mark Zandi, chief economist for Moody's Economy.com, see the bailout as a success. "When you take the totality of what was done here, it saved the global financial system and ensured that the Great Recession did not turn into a depression."[15] Nevertheless, in 2010, the number of home foreclosures reached 1 million for the first time in US history and lending remains constricted. University of Texas economics professor James K. Galbraith claims that the bailout achieved success at a price, "forestalling a restructuring and reform that would get at the root of the financial crises."[16] Also in 2010, Wall Street's large firms posted record earnings while the nation's unemployment rate remained at nearly 10 percent. Due to these disparities, the bailout debate remains hotly contested, as the divergent viewpoints in At Issue: Are Government Bailouts Effective? make clear.

14. Norman Ornstein, "Ornstein on the Economy's Moral Hazard Meltdown," New Republic, October 8, 2008.
15. Quoted in Don Gonya, "TARP Puts Some Republicans on the Defensive," NPR, June 30, 2010.
16. James K. Galbraith, "The Great Crisis and the American Response," keynote address to the German American Association for American Studies, Berlin, May 27, 2010.

1

The Bank Bailout Prevented Global Economic Collapse

Fareed Zakaria

Fareed Zakaria is editor of Newsweek International, *host of CNN's international affairs program* Fareed Zakaria GPS, *and author of* The Post-American World.

The US government's financial bailout prevented global economic collapse. The failure of Lehman Brothers, a global investment bank, shocked lawmakers into taking action to stabilize the financial system. When Lehman went bankrupt, banks stopped lending. Production fell and millions of people lost their jobs. However, the knowledge that the government would inject money into the system restored confidence. Indeed, the fact that people think the bailout was unnecessary is evidence that it worked. While asking taxpayers to bail out rich banks that behaved irresponsibly is unconscionable, government intervention was necessary to save the economy. Nevertheless, lawmakers must address the deeper problems facing the nation to prevent future crises.

September is the month for anniversaries from hell. Last week [mid-September 2010] we remembered 9/11, and this week it's time to recall the collapse of Lehman Brothers [a large investment bank]. Most of the discussion about the financial crisis has focused on a question that won't go away: could the fall of Lehman have been prevented? For many this was the cardinal error that sparked the crisis. Others believe that Lehman was the precipitating factor, but that the financial system was so highly leveraged that something or other would eventually have broken its back.

Stabilizing the Financial System

We will never know what would have happened if Lehman had not failed. But we can be fairly sure that without its collapse, it would have been impossible to shock the political system into action. In the month after the fall, the U.S. government made a series of massive moves to restore stability to the financial system. And it's clear that those actions saved the American—and thus the global—economy from total collapse.

The contraction in global trade in late 2008 and early 2009 was worse than in 1929 and 1930. In other words, we were surely headed for something that looked like a Great Depression.

Consider the facts. After the fall of Lehman, credit froze in the U.S. economy. Banks stopped lending to anyone, even Fortune 500 companies with gold-plated credit. People couldn't get consumer and car loans at any price, businesses couldn't get short-term loans to meet payroll. Private-sector borrowing—the lifeblood of modern economies—fell from 15 percent of GDP [gross domestic product] in late 2007 to minus 1 percent of GDP in late 2008.

The effects on the broader economy were immediate. GDP shrank by 6 percent in one quarter. Some 1.7 million people lost their jobs, the biggest drop in employment in 65 years, which was then exceeded in the next quarter when 2.1 million jobs evaporated. The net worth of American households decreased by $5 trillion, falling at the unprecedented rate of 30 percent a year. The worldwide numbers did not look much better. The contraction in global trade in late 2008 and early

2009 was worse than in 1929 and 1930. In other words, we were surely headed for something that looked like a Great Depression.

Restoring Confidence

The U.S. government's actions stopped the fall. Between the passage of the Troubled Asset Relief Program (TARP) and the massive quantitative easing of the Federal Reserve, markets realized that the government was backstopping the financial system, that credit was beginning to flow again, and that if no one else was going to inject capital into the system, the U.S. government would do so. Part substance, part symbolism, the effect was to restore confidence and stability to the system. In fact, the financial system bounced back so fast that the government will likely recover almost 90 percent of the funds it committed during those months, making this one of the cheapest financial bailouts in history.

The best evidence that TARP worked is that now, most people think it was unnecessary. In fact, about 60 percent of the country thinks it was a bad idea. Congressmen and senators who supported it now distance themselves; the most powerful line of attack against any of them tends to be that they voted for the bailouts. JFK said that victory has 100 fathers, and defeat is an orphan. But this is the strange case of a success that no one wants to claim.

We had to save the banks to save the economy.

Practical Realities

Bank bailouts have always been unpopular. People hate to pay the bills for other people's improvidence, and they detest having to do so for rich people. Viewed in moral terms, TARP is unconscionable. Financial institutions created the mess, and yet they were the ones being bailed out. But governance is sometimes about practical realities. Had the financial system gone under, the American economy would have come to a standstill. It very nearly did. We had to save the banks to save the economy.

The remarkable aspect of TARP, in retrospect, was the bipartisanship that made it possible. Hank Paulson and Barney Frank became comrades in arms. George W. Bush cooperated with Nancy Pelosi. Conservative Republicans endorsed a vast government appropriation. Liberal Democrats supported a bank bailout. The fact that people of wildly differing political persuasions all came to the conclusion that this was the right policy should be some proof that it was not ideologically motivated. For a moment in September 2008, Washington worked.

Alas, it won't happen again. It took a crisis to concentrate the minds of politicians. The American system had a heart attack and we responded fast and well. Unfortunately, the problems we face in the future are less like heart attacks and more like cancer—problems that if unattended will grow and metastasize. In the long run, though, they'll have the same effect on the patient.

2

The Bank Bailout Failed to Make Wall Street Accountable

Monika Bauerlein and Clara Jeffery

Monika Bauerlein and Clara Jeffery are co-editors of Mother Jones, *an investigative news magazine.*

Financial bailouts reward irresponsible behavior and fail to make large investment banks accountable. Indeed, while millions of Americans have lost homes and jobs, bank executives continue to profit from bailout money. More appalling is the revelation that these bankers feel no remorse. Moreover, many Americans blame politicians, not the bankers who convinced the public that the government should not regulate financial institutions. Thus, big banks acted without restraint and dealt in risky financial instruments, believing the bubble would never burst. When it did, consumers were the ones who suffered and learned to act with more restraint while the bankers responsible for the financial crises are back to business as usual.

Maybe Wall Street should open a casino right there on the corner of Broad, because these guys simply cannot lose. After kneecapping the global economy, costing millions their homes and livelihoods, and saddling our grandchildren with massive debt—after all that, they're cashing in their bonuses from 2008. That's right, 2008—when amid the gnashing of teeth and rending of garments over the $700 billion TARP [Troubled Asset Relief Program] legislation (a mere 5 percent

Monika Bauerlein and Clara Jeffery, "Too Big to Jail? Time to Fix Wall Street's Accountability Deficit," *Mother Jones*, January/February 2010. © 2010, Foundation for National Progress. All rights reserved. Reproduced with permission.

of a $14 trillion bailout), humiliated banks rolled back executive bonuses. Or so we thought: In fact, those bonuses were simply reconfigured to have a higher proportion of company stock. Those shares weren't worth so much at the time, as the execs made a point of telling Congress, but that meant they could only go up, and by the time they did, the public (suckers!) would have forgotten the whole exercise. It worked out beautifully: The value of [global financial service firm] JP-Morgan Chase's 2008 bonuses has increased 20 percent to $10.5 billion, an average of nearly $6 million for the top 200 execs. [Global financial service firm] Goldman's 2008 bonuses are worth $7.8 billion.

Rewarding bad behavior produces more of the same—so it's no surprise that Wall Street is back to business as usual.

Rewarding Bad Behavior

And why are bank stocks worth more now? Because of the bailout, of course. Bankers aren't being rewarded for pulling the economy out of the doldrums. Nope, they're simply skimming from the trillions we've shoveled at them. The house always wins. Indeed, 2009 bonuses are expected to be 30 to 40 percent higher than 2008's. And don't forget AIG [an insurance and investment firm], which paid the same division who helped cook up collateral debt obligations and credit default swaps "retention bonuses" worth $475 million, in some execs' cases 36 times their base salaries.

As anyone who watches *Dog Whisperer* knows, rewarding bad behavior produces more of the same—so it's no surprise that Wall Street is back to business as usual. Derivatives are still unregulated (thanks, Congress!), exotic sliced-and-diced securities are being resliced and rediced, and the biggest offenders in peddling subprime mortgages? They are raking in millions in federal grants to—wait for it—fix subprime mortgages.

No Remorse

And the worst part? These fat-cat recidivists don't even have the decency to fake contrition. The *New York Times'* Andrew Ross Sorkin says that whenever he asked Wall Street CEOs "Do you have any remorse? Are you sorry? The answer, almost unequivocally, was no." When asked by Mojo's [*Mother Jones'*] Stephanie Mencimer if he regretted helping to bring down the economy, former AIG CEO Hank Greenberg said flatly, "No. I think we had a very good record." Lloyd Blankfein, Goldman Sachs' CEO (his haul between 2006–2008: $157 million) went so far as to tell the *Times* of London, "We help companies to grow by helping them to raise capital. It's a virtuous cycle. We have a social purpose." Bankers like him are "doing God's work."

This is blasphemy worthy—along with usury—of the 7th circle of hell. And while Goldman's PR minions, visions of pitch-forks dancing in their heads, coaxed Blankfein into coughing up a lame apology, the comment perfectly distilled the Kool-Aid[1] Wall Street has forced down our throats. Mojo's Kevin Dram sums it up in his investigation of Wall Street's outsize influence in Washington: Political payola—$475 million in campaign contributions just in the 2008 cycle—is only part of it. Something more insidious is at work. "Unlike most industries, which everyone recognizes are merely lobbying in their own self-interest, the finance industry successfully convinced everyone that deregulating finance was not only safe, but self-evidently good for the entire economy, Wall Street and Main Street alike," he writes. Some call this phenomenon

---

1. Here Kool-Aid is a metaphor for the unquestioning belief in an ideology, argument, or philosophy without critical examination.

"intellectual capture," he adds, but "considering what's happened over the past couple of years, we might better call it Stockholm syndrome."[2]

When it comes to restraint and humility, consumers seem to be the only ones learning their lesson.

Putting Blame Where It Belongs

Sure enough, as our Washington bureau chief David Corn reports, pollsters have been surprised to find that while Americans are angry about the economy, they often blame not the bankers, but politicians—and even themselves. We spent too much, the logic goes, and now we're reaping the rewards. There's some validity to that—we all played along as if the good times would never end. But who sold us this crock? Wall Street and its troubadours, from faux regulators like Alan Greenspan to so-called financial journalists like Jim "Mad Dog" Cramer.

And actually, when it comes to restraint and humility, consumers seem to be the only ones learning their lesson. Personal savings are up for the first time in decades; spending is down. Why? Because we, the little people, actually felt the pain of the crash. New incentives, new behavior. Not so on Wall Street; not so in Washington.

It's not too late. If nothing else, last summer's tea parties showed that politicians will listen to popular outrage—when it seems to threaten their jobs. What if, as Nobel-winning economist Joe Stiglitz suggests, we foreclosed on bankers and politicians who are morally bankrupt? What if people started showing up at town halls demanding accountability from those who gambled away their jobs and homes? There is plenty of blame to go around. Let's start putting some of it back where it belongs.

2. Stockholm syndrome is a psychological phenomenon in which hostages express empathy for and have positive feelings towards their captors.

3

Repaid Bailout Debt Has Not Benefited Taxpayers

Howard Rich

Howard Rich is chairman and founder of Americans for Limited Government, an organization that supports free market principles and individual rights and advocates reducing the role of government in individual affairs.

Although lawmakers are congratulating themselves on saving the economy by passing the Troubled Asset Relief Program, no evidence shows that taxpayers will benefit. Moreover, saving the big banks did not prevent the financial crises that left millions of Americans unemployed and others with less income. In truth, whether the government will profit from its investment in troubled financial institutions is debatable. Nevertheless, the problem is not a matter of accounting but principles. Even if these taxpayer-funded investments do yield a return, it does not mean taxpayers will benefit. The government will likely spend this money on more bailouts, not to reduce America's debt.

As the infamous Troubled Asset Relief Program (TARP) winds down this week [early October 2010], Republicans and Democrats in Washington, D.C. are patting themselves on the back for a job well done. Not only are they claiming to have saved the nation from a "Second Great Depression," this so-called economic miracle was apparently purchased at a bargain basement price.

Howard Rich, "The 'Toxic' Truth About TARP," *NetRightDaily*, October 9, 2010. All rights reserved. Reproduced with permission.

According to the Congressional Budget Office, TARP will cost taxpayers "only" $66 billion. The White House puts the figure even lower—at $50 billion.

Of course these rosy, election-year estimates are based on government liquidating its ownership stake in hundreds of "private" corporations—including a 92 percent stake in the [insurance and investment firm] American International Group (AIG) and a 61 percent stake in General Motors (GM).

A Daunting Task

For taxpayers to recoup their "investment" in AIG, the government will have to sell 1.66 billion shares of common stock at an average price of $29 per share. At GM, the government must sell 304 million shares of common stock at an average price of nearly $134 per share. Hitting these targets would be a daunting task in any economic climate—and may prove insurmountable in our ongoing malaise.

"How does one get $49 billion out of a company that's currently worth $25 billion?" an investment research publication recently asked. "The follow on question is: why would investors buy AIG shares while the government's AIG stock sale could last 18–24 months?"

Short answer? They wouldn't—and likely won't.

Meanwhile GM has dramatically scaled back its initial public offering in recent weeks—a sign that the company will be forced to continue operating under the "Government Motors" banner for the foreseeable future.

But this debate isn't about getting an accurate accounting of the final TARP tab and assessing its risk versus reward—it's about honestly assessing the problems that come with government picking winners and losers in the marketplace in the first place. Even if government's taxpayer-funded investments yielded better than average returns (or huge cash windfalls), that doesn't make them right—nor does it mean taxpayers will ever see one red cent of their money back.

And while TARP has enabled union bosses in Detroit and AIG executives ail over the world to make out like bandits (as bureaucrats across the country did in the wake of the "stimulus"), what about the people who were forced to pick up the tab? What about the 15 million Americans who are currently unemployed? Or the millions of American households that have seen their income levels decline in each of the last two years? What about the small business owners whose taxes are about to skyrocket as government begins making interest payments on its massive new debt?

Certainly interest rates are low for the time being, but the threat of rising rates is a ticking time bomb.

In designating the wealthiest Wall Street banks as "too big to fail" Washington told the rest of America that it was "too small to succeed."

None of the TARP money that's been repaid to the U.S. government thus far is actually being returned to taxpayers. Nor is it being used to pay down America's ballooning debt.

Questioning the Doom and Gloom

Also, there is also considerable debate as to the accuracy of the "doom and gloom" pronouncements that preceded TARP—which would obviously negate much of its supposed efficacy in avoiding a global economic meltdown.

For example, a week before TARP passed Federal Reserve Chairman Ben Bernanke appeared before the Joint Economic Committee of the U.S. Congress and made an impassioned plea for taxpayer-funded intervention, saying that emergency action was required immediately in order to "address the grave threats to financial stability that we currently face."

At this hearing, Bernanke testified that the commercial paper market was on the verge of shutting down. This sent major shock waves through Congress, as many companies use the sale of this short-term debt to pay their bills and make payroll. A week after Congress passed TARP, however, Bernanke announced the creation of a special commercial paper funding facility—thus arbitrarily alleviating one of the key pressures he had used as leverage to help get the bailout passed.

Perhaps the most effective argument against those who claimed that the sky would fall in October 2008 absent government intervention is the fact that government intervened—and the sky fell anyway. Economists in their taxpayer-funded ivory towers will no doubt continue to do battle over hypothetical contingencies, but that doesn't change the fact that 8 million jobs vanished in just over a year's time—and those jobs aren't coming back anytime soon.

Meanwhile, none of the TARP money that's been repaid to the U.S. government thus far is actually being returned to taxpayers. Nor is it being used to pay down America's ballooning debt. Instead, it's being spent on new bailouts, more borrowing and additional deficit spending.

Also, in confronting the "toxic" realities of TARP it's important to remember that its initial $700 billion outlay represents only a small sliver of the money government has spent, lent, pledged and printed since the recession began in December 2007.

That's a tab taxpayers will still be picking up decades from now.

4

The Bank Bailout Failed to Achieve Its Broader Goals

Neil M. Barofsky

Neil M. Barofsky was the special inspector general for the Troubled Asset Relief Program from 2008 until 2011 and is currently a senior fellow at the New York University Center on the Administration of Criminal Law.

Although the big bank bailout prevented financial collapse, the Troubled Asset Relief Program (TARP) failed to meet many of its goals—goals that encouraged reluctant lawmakers to vote in favor of the program. For example, TARP failed to compel banks to increase lending to homebuyers. In addition, the program fell short of its goal to modify the mortgages of millions of families struggling to make their mortgage payments. Nor did regulatory reforms to prevent the reckless behavior of large banks materialize. In fact, many big banks are even larger and have no incentive to avoid risky banking practices. As a result, TARP failed to keep its promise to protect American homeowners and is viewed as nothing more than a Wall Street handout.

Two and a half years ago [September 2008], Congress passed the legislation that bailed out the country's banks. The government has declared its mission accomplished, calling the program remarkably effective "by any objective measure." On my last day as the special inspector general of the bailout program, I regret to say that I strongly disagree. The bank bailout, more formally called the Troubled Asset Relief Program [TARP], failed to meet some of its most important goals.

From the perspective of the largest financial institutions, the glowing assessment is warranted: billions of dollars in taxpayer money allowed institutions that were on the brink of collapse not only to survive but even to flourish. These banks now enjoy record profits and the seemingly permanent competitive advantage that accompanies being deemed "too big to fail."

Broader Goals

Though there is no question that the country benefited by avoiding a meltdown of the financial system, this cannot be the only yardstick by which TARP's legacy is measured. The legislation that created TARP, the Emergency Economic Stabilization Act, had far broader goals, including protecting home values and preserving homeownership.

These Main Street-oriented goals were not, as the Treasury Department is now suggesting, mere window dressing that needed only to be taken "into account." Rather, they were a central part of the compromise with reluctant members of Congress to cast a vote that in many cases proved to be political suicide.

Almost immediately, . . . Treasury's plan for TARP shifted from the purchase of mortgages to the infusion of hundreds of billions of dollars into the nation's largest financial institutions.

The act's emphasis on preserving homeownership was particularly vital to passage. Congress was told that TARP would be used to purchase up to $700 billion of mortgages, and, to obtain the necessary votes, Treasury promised that it would modify those mortgages to assist struggling homeowners. Indeed, the act expressly directs the department to do just that.

But it has done little to abide by this legislative bargain. Almost immediately, as permitted by the broad language of the act, Treasury's plan for TARP shifted from the purchase of mortgages to the infusion of hundreds of billions of dollars into the nation's largest financial institutions, a shift that came with the express promise that it would restore lending.

Failing to Help Homeowners

Treasury, however, provided the money to banks with no effective policy or effort to compel the extension of credit. There were no strings attached: no requirement or even incentive to increase lending to home buyers, and against our strong recommendation, not even a request that banks report how they used TARP funds. It was only in April of last year, in response to recommendations from our office, that Treasury asked banks to provide that information, well after the largest banks had already repaid their loans. It was therefore no surprise that lending did not increase but rather continued to decline well into the recovery. (In my job as special inspector general I could not bring about the changes I thought were needed—I could only make recommendations to the Treasury Department.)

Meanwhile, the act's goal of helping struggling homeowners was shelved until February 2009, when the Home Affordable Modification Program was announced with the promise to help up to four million families with mortgage modifications.

That program has been a colossal failure, with far fewer permanent modifications (540,000) than modifications that have failed and been canceled (over 800,000). This is the well-chronicled result of the rush to get the program started, major program design flaws like the failure to remedy mortgage servicers' favoring of foreclosure over permanent modifications, and a refusal to hold those abysmally performing mortgage servicers accountable for their disregard of program guidelines. As the program flounders, foreclosures continue to mount, with 8 million to 13 million filings forecast over the program's lifetime.

Treasury Secretary Timothy Geithner has acknowledged that the program "won't come close" to fulfilling its original expectations, that its incentives are not "powerful enough" and that the mortgage servicers are "still doing a terribly inadequate job." But Treasury officials refuse to address these shortfalls. Instead they continue to stubbornly maintain that the program is a success and needs no material change, effectively assuring that Treasury's most specific Main Street promise will not be honored.

It has been Treasury's broken promises that have turned TARP . . . into a program commonly viewed as little more than a giveaway to Wall Street executives.

No Real Regulatory Reform

Finally, the country was assured that regulatory reform would address the threat to our financial system posed by large banks that have become effectively guaranteed by the government no matter how reckless their behavior. This promise also appears likely to go unfulfilled. The biggest banks are 20 percent larger than they were before the crisis and control a larger part of our economy than ever. They reasonably assume that the government will rescue them again, if necessary. Indeed, credit rating agencies incorporate future government bailouts into their assessments of the largest banks, exaggerating market distortions that provide them with an unfair advantage over smaller institutions, which continue to struggle.

Worse, Treasury apparently has chosen to ignore rather than support real efforts at reform, such as those advocated by

Sheila Bair, the chairwoman of the Federal Deposit Insurance Corporation, to simplify or shrink the most complex financial institutions.

In the final analysis, it has been Treasury's broken promises that have turned TARP—which was instrumental in saving the financial system at a relatively modest cost to taxpayers—into a program commonly viewed as little more than a giveaway to Wall Street executives.

It wasn't meant to be that. Indeed, Treasury's mismanagement of TARP and its disregard for TARP's Main Street goals—whether born of incompetence, timidity in the face of a crisis or a mindset too closely aligned with the banks it was supposed to rein in—may have so damaged the credibility of the government as a whole that future policy makers maybe politically unable to take the necessary steps to save the system the next time a crisis arises. This avoidable political reality might just be TARP's most lasting, and unfortunate, legacy.

5

Bailing Out the Big Banks Was Unfair to Smaller Banks

Frank Lucas

Frank Lucas, a Republican representative from Oklahoma, is a senior member of the House Financial Services Committee.

The big bank bailout that protected many of those financial institutions responsible for the financial crises left smaller banks unprotected. Instead of making big banks smaller and thus no longer "too big to fail," the bailout made them stronger, giving them a competitive advantage over small banks. In addition, small banks have to pay for the mistakes of these large investment banks in the form of emergency fees. Small banks will have to pass these fees along, which not only punishes good customers but makes these banks even less competitive. Financial reforms should help the blameless small institutions that are critical to economic recovery by helping them become more competitive.

Last week [mid-September 2009] marked the one-year anniversary of the collapse of Lehman Brothers [a large financial investment bank] and the beginning of Washington's unprecedented intervention in our financial markets. Since then, the federal government has spent $180 billion bailing out insurance giant AIG, followed by government-imposed takeovers and mergers of some of our country's largest banks and financial institutions, the controversial $700 billion bank bailout plan, and the $81 billion bailout of Detroit automakers. This means, within the last year, the federal government has spent almost $1 trillion of American taxpayers' money bailing out those large financial institutions on Wall Street who made irresponsible choices, claiming these companies pose a systemic risk and are "too big to fail."

Smaller banks that were also suffering from the credit crunch that was caused by many of those same financial institutions the Treasury bailed out . . . were left to fend for themselves or to fail.

Yet, rather than taking steps to ensure that "too big to fail" companies no longer posed such a massive risk to our financial system, the Obama administration has actually taken steps to make these companies even larger. After the Treasury Department strong-armed Bank of America into purchasing Merrill Lynch, and JP Morgan Chase into purchasing Bear Stearns, these two "superbanks" now hold more than $2 of every $10 deposited. And, combined, four of the largest financial institutions in the country—Bank of America, JP Morgan Chase, Wells Fargo, and Citigroup—issue one of every two mortgages and two of every three credit cards in this country.

Small Banks Must Fend for Themselves

Then came the $700 billion bailout. Rather than spending the money to purchase illiquid assets in an effort to free up credit and restore liquidity in the market as we were told, the Treasury Department used much of the first $350 billion allotted to bail out the largest financial institutions on the East and West coasts. And for the smaller banks that were also suffering from the credit crunch that was caused by many of those same financial institutions the Treasury bailed out? They were left to fend for themselves or to fail.

As these massive financial conglomerates—propped up by billions of federal dollars—grow larger, the uneven playing field that already exists between large and small banks continues to expand.

To begin with, community banks were held responsible for the risky mistakes made on Wall Street by the Federal Deposit Insurance Company. As banks began to fail, the FDIC coffers began to clear. An emergency fee was assessed on all banks—even those who had very little to do with the current financial crisis and who have continued to serve their communities well through these troubled times.

And the FDIC announced earlier this month that it would substantially increase the fees banks pay to insure their holdings. While large financial institutions are more able to cushion the blow of these higher fees—especially since many are still operating on billions of dollars from the federal government—small, community banks will have a much more difficult time paying these new assessments.

Burdening Local Banks

In yet another move that will disproportionately harm small banks, House Financial Services Committee Chairman Barney Frank (D-Mass.) and President Obama recently announced their intentions to create the Consumer Financial Protection Agency. Don't let this name mislead you. This dangerous piece of legislation will actually do more harm to consumers than good. The additional bureaucratic red tape, fees, and government intervention this agency will create will do nothing but decrease the availability of credit and increase the cost of goods and services. This agency will excessively burden local banks, which will have a much more difficult time than large financial institutions with handling the additional costs and regulations that will come with this new agency.

With all these additional fees and costs, community banks could be forced to raise the fees they charge their customers.

This not only punishes their loyal customers; it can also make the banks less competitive within our financial system and could potentially drive some out of business all together.

I guess the Obama administration's policy of "too big to fail" really means "too small to matter."

If there is one thing my constituents made clear to me at the 18 town hall meetings I held during the month of August, it was this: Americans are tired of bailing out Wall Street. As a senior member of the House Financial Services Committee, I will continue to encourage President Obama and Chairman Frank to reconsider their approach to reforming our financial system. I do not deny that some changes within our system are necessary. However, when considering how best to approach reform, we must not sacrifice the health of our small institutions that did not cause the current crisis and are critical to our country's economic recovery.

6

Repealing Commercial and Investment Banking Separation Led to the Bailout

Thomas Frank

Thomas Frank, now a columnist for Harper's Magazine, *was for many years a regular columnist for the* Wall Street Journal. *He is author of* One Market Under God: Extreme Capitalism, Market Populism, and the End of Economic Democracy.

The mythical belief that an unregulated financial market would bring unlimited prosperity came to end with the 2008 financial crisis. In fact, some lawmakers are recommending regulatory policies that separate commercial and more risky investment banking services. Nevertheless, many continue to dismiss as antiquated any laws that resemble Glass-Steagall, a 1933 law, for the most part repealed in 1999, that separated investment and commercial banking during the economic crises of the Great Depression. However, ignoring the value of such regulation is as risky as trusting that the big banks could not fail. A separation must exist between government guaranteed commercial banks and investment banks that take big risks.

Last month [December 2009], Sens. Maria Cantwell and John McCain proposed a measure that would revive parts of the old Glass-Steagall Act, the 1933 law that separated investment from commercial banking. After having been diluted many times over the years, Glass-Steagall was largely repealed in 1999, permitting a wave of consolidation in the financial industry.

The latest [financial] crisis [that began with the 2008 collapse of Lehman Brothers, a large investment bank] has provoked a new debate over the old regulatory regime. Nobel laureate economist Joseph Stiglitz has argued that the repeal of Glass-Steagall had an "especial role" in making the financial calamity of 2008 possible. Former Fed [Federal Reserve] Chairman Paul Volcker, currently the head of the President's Economic Recovery Advisory Board, has called for a new separation between commercial banking and riskier financial activities.

A Powerful Stereotype

Any discussion about breaking up the financial industry, however, runs into a powerful stereotype: the overwhelming consensus belief in the risible backwardness of Glass-Steagall.

In 1999, the last time the 1933 law was being debated, it was routinely described as a "Depression-era" law, a "relic" of a benighted age, "venerable," "obsolete," "outdated," "archaic," insufficient to meet the public's "sophisticated needs" in the bold new era of accelerated everything. The measure that overturned Glass-Steagall in 1999 was, of course, called the "Financial Services Modernization Act."

Having government forbid everyday commercial banks to take gambles on high-risk schemes, why, that just didn't make sense to the enlightened minds of 1999. We had learned by then to trust the market. Besides, what could go wrong? Fears about speculative risk were so 1933!

Today, it is that old critique of Glass-Steagall that strikes one as a relic in need of modernization. Reading through journalistic accounts of the old regulatory regime from 1999 is like watching long reels of ecstatic dot-com commercials or flipping through the metallic-and-fluorescent pages of old copies of *Wired* magazine and remembering the mind-blowing prosperity that the Internet was supposed to be bringing us.

The "New Economy" Mysticism

The business-culture delusions of the '90s may seem obvious today. But at the time, our great thinkers assured us that we had turned a historical corner and the "old rules" no longer applied. Prosperity was eternal. And government was a dinosaur, serving only to impede our pursuit of info-age excellence. Again and again, the narrow agenda of particular interests were cast as freedom for all of humanity.

Consider "The Twilight of Sovereignty," the influential 1992 manifesto by former Citicorp CEO Walter Wriston. Here was a man who had spent much of his career warring against Glass-Steagall and other federal banking regulations. In his book, however, he did not criticize regulation so that Citi might be permitted to become a grotesquely distended too-big-to-fail financial supermarket gambling in whatever schemes would bring the richest bonuses. Certainly not. Wriston instructed us to give up on regulation because we had entered a new stage of history and regulation was now technologically obsolete. "How does [government] track or control the money supply when the financial markets create new financial instruments faster than the regulators can keep track of them?" he asked.

Half-baked historicism like that was persuasive stuff in those days. On the occasion of the old banking law's repeal, President Bill Clinton intoned that Glass-Steagall was "no longer appropriate to the economy in which we live. It worked pretty well for the industrial economy. . . . But the world is very different."

Today, as we begin to debate Glass-Steagall all over again, the old stereotypes are simply being pulled out of deep-freeze. The futility of efforts to "turn back the clock" are noted. A clever put-down from an anonymous Treasury official is much repeated: it "would be like going back to the Walkman."

The old law's revival is said to be a way of pandering to the low emotions of the public, as opposed to its higher faculties of reason. A *Business Week* story on the subject understands the Cantwell-McCain proposal as a way of "soothing public anger over bailouts and bonuses." Politico's account of the measure chalks the whole thing up to "populist angst," whatever that is.

The answer involves . . . drawing a line between banks that the government effectively guarantees and banks that behave like big hedge funds, experimenting with the latest financial toxins.

What no one has yet grasped is that pooh-poohing Glass-Steagall in this way is about as sound a move as was slapping down your savings on shares of TheGlobe.com.[1]

One of these days, we will finally dispel the "New Economy" mysticism that beclouds this issue and begin to think seriously about how to re-regulate the financial sector. And when we do, we may find that the answer involves some version of the idea behind Glass-Steagall—drawing a line between banks that the government effectively guarantees and banks that behave like big hedge funds, experimenting with the latest financial toxins. Hopefully, that day will come before Wall Street decides to take another headlong run at some attractive cliff.

---

1. TheGlobe.com was a social networking service that made headlines by going public on November 1998 and posting the largest first day gain of any initial public offering in history to that date. The CEO became a symbol of the excesses of dot-com millionaires during the dot-com bubble, in which new Interest-based companies saw a significant rise in stock prices. By 2001 a majority of these companies ceased trading after using up their venture capital without having made a net profit. Investors often referred to these failed dot-coms as "dot-bombs."

7

Political and Not Economic Concerns Motivated Bank Bailout Legislation

Jim F. Couch, Mark D. Foster, Keith Malone, and David L. Black

Jim F. Couch is professor of economics, Mark D. Foster is associate professor of finance, Keith Malone is associate professor of economics, and David L. Black is an economics instructor at the University of North Alabama.

Because lawmakers feared that support for the financial bailout program might mean political suicide, they sought to assure their constituents that the program would protect American values and save the economy from collapse. However, a study of those who voted in favor of the bailout reveals that political considerations in fact motivated the vote of most lawmakers. In the House, long-serving Democrats who had received financial service sector political contributions were more likely to vote in favor of the bailout. In the Senate, while party did not seem to have any influence, those with more years of service who received financial service sector political contributions were more likely to vote in favor of the bailout bill. Clearly, investment-banking interests exert too much influence in Congress and, unfortunately, Americans pay the price.

Jim F. Couch, Mark D. Foster, Keith Malone, and David L. Black, "An Analysis of the Financial Services Bailout Vote," *Cato Journal*, Vol. 31, No. 1, Winter 2011. All rights reserved. Reproduced with permission.

Washington's remedy to the financial problems that began in 2008 was the Troubled Asset Relief Program (TARP)—the so-called bailout of the banking system. Whatever its merits, it was, for the most part, unpopular with the American public. Lawmakers, fearful that the economy might actually collapse without some action, were likewise fearful that action—in the form of a payout to the Wall Street financiers—would prove to be harmful to them at the polls. Thus, politicians sought to assure the public that their vote on the measure would reflect Main Street virtues, not Wall Street greed.

Members of Congress, addressing the public's misgivings about the bailout, asserted that they were wrestling with difficult issues such as fairness and equity, banking regulation, executive pay, job losses, moral hazard, 401(k) values, and the proper role of the state. Furthermore, they argued, these complex issues were difficult for the public to understand, and legislators, vigilant in carrying out their duty, were weighing the pros and the cons in order to cast a vote that was in the best interest of the nation.

But it turns out that when one moves beyond the speeches, the underlying motivation behind most votes cast was hardly complex and actually quite simple. In this article, we construct a model to analyze the bailout vote of each legislator. A simple reelection model of legislator behavior explains a majority of the votes taken either for or against the measure from politician to politician.

Wall Street vs. Main Street

Those with an appreciation of the merits of limited government enjoy reflecting on the past. They recall those halcyon days when a balanced budget amendment—a rather quant notion by today's standards—failed by only a single vote in the Senate. How things have changed.

The economic zeitgeist [the spirit of the times] is government takeovers, bailouts, and stimulus plans along with escalating debt and deficits. Indeed, commenting on the federal budget for FY 2009, Stanford University economist Michael Boskin (2009) put government borrowing in perspective: "The budget more than doubles the national debt held by the public, adding more to the debt than all previous presidents— from George Washington to George W. Bush—combined." Indeed, the FY 2009 budget deficit was larger than the entire economy of India and almost as much as the Canadian economy. [According to M. Crutsinger (2009)], "Forecasts of more red ink mean the federal government is heading toward spending 15 percent of its money by 2019 just to pay interest on the debt, up from 5 percent this fiscal year."

Congress, fearful that the economy might actually collapse without the bailout but aware that rewarding Wall Street would agitate voters, did what they do best—they made speeches appealing to populism.

It could be argued, however, that the staggering explosion of federal debt under the Obama administration was precipitated by unprecedented spending during the Bush administration. The Emergency Economic Stabilization Act of 2008, otherwise known as TARP, whatever its merits in terms of rescuing the economy, represented a dramatic departure from normal government operations. As President Bush all but acknowledged in his November 12, 2009, address at Southern Methodist University, TARP opened the floodgates of government intrusion into the private sector:

I went against my free-market instincts and approved a temporary government intervention to unfreeze credit and prevent a global financial catastrophe. . . . As the world recovers, we will face a temptation to replace the risk-and-reward model of the private sector with the blunt instruments of government spending and control. History shows that the greater threat to prosperity is not too little government involvement, but too much.

The $700 billion dollar stabilization package was designed to provide liquidity to the nation's banking and financial firms that faced, at best, uncertain futures. Assisting the financial industry through taxpayer loans and grants proved to be unpopular with the American public.

Jonathan Weisman, writing in the *Washington Post*, acknowledged the unusual nature of the vote: "Rarely has a congressional vote held such high drama and produced such immediate repercussions, directly from the House floor to the trading floor."

Appealing to Populism

Congress, fearful that the economy might actually collapse without the bailout but aware that rewarding Wall Street would agitate voters, did what they do best—they made speeches appealing to populism. Most castigated Wall Street greed, differentiating between Main Street virtue and Wall Street avarice. Others took aim at Treasury Secretary Henry Paulson. Representative Brad Sherman (D-CA) provides a useful example:

> We live in an era of great concentration of power in the Executive Branch and great concentration of wealth on Wall Street. Today we are asked to approve the greatest power grab any executive has ever asked for and the greatest transfer of wealth Wall Street could imagine. . . . We can make a bill that reflects American values and not Wall Street values.

Senator Sherrod Brown (D-OH) acknowledged the public's displeasure with TARP: "I don't think a single call to my office on this proposal has been positive. I don't think I have gotten one yet of the literally thousands of emails and calls we're getting" (Brown 2008).

Representative Peter DeFazio (D-OR) criticized Wall Street but, in addition, attacked Secretary Paulson directly:

> He wants to take care of Wall Street's illiquid assets, as what he nicely labels them. Nice charitable pundits have said Cash for Trash. Wall Street could then return to business as usual. That is Mr. Paulson's plan. He is of, by, for and about Wall Street, former head of Goldman Sachs. We should not be rolled by a Wall Street exec who is masquerading as Secretary of the Treasury.

Senator Chris Dodd (D-CT), chairman of the Senate Banking Committee, echoed the Wall Street versus Main Street theme and pointed out who was likely to benefit from the expenditures:

> It would do nothing, in my view, to help a single family save a home, at least not upfront. It would do nothing to stop even a single CEO from dumping billions of dollars of toxic assets on the backs of American taxpayers, while at the same time do nothing to stop the very authors of this calamity to walk away with bonuses and golden parachutes worth millions of dollars.

Richard Shelby (R-AL) agreed with his Democratic colleagues, asserting:

> The Treasury's plan has little for those outside of the financial industry. It is aimed at rescuing the same financial institutions that created this crisis, with the sloppy underwriting and reckless disregard for the risks they were creating, taking or passing on to others. Wall Street bet that the government would rescue them if they got into trouble. It appears that bet may be the one that pays off.

Lawmakers unequivocally pronounced that Wall Street elites would not win the day. It was made clear that Main Street had the ear of the Congress. Taxpayers would not bear the brunt of the miscalculations of the bankers, brokers, and financiers.

The Government Allocation of TARP Funds

A few politicians were uncomfortable with the expanded role that government was playing in the market. Representative William Thornberry (R-TX) made this observation and pointed out that he had wrestled with the issue:

> Deciding how to vote on this issue has been among the most difficult votes I have cast in Congress. The economic condition and well-being of every American will be affected. I continue to be uncomfortable with the degree of government intrusion into our economy that this bill would authorize. I also continue to be concerned about the economic consequences to all Americans if some sort of action is not taken. It is balancing those two positions that make this vote extremely difficult.

While we are admittedly getting a little ahead of ourselves, Representative Thornberry's fears proved to be valid. The bailout vote did indeed pass, but the funds were not directed in a manner consistent with an effort to increase liquidity—and thereby, hopefully, bring about recovery. Instead, funds were directed to financial institutions with political clout.

Empirical evidence . . . shows a systematic political component to the distribution of TARP funds.

Bank Ties to Legislators

Healthy banks that could make loans and supply liquidity were supposed to receive TARP funds in order to head off financial calamity. OneUnited Bank certainly did not meet that requirement. The bank was in deep trouble. However, the bank was tied to two powerful legislators: Congressman Barney Frank (D-MA) and Congresswoman Maxine Waters (D-CA). Both Frank and Waters served on the House Financial Services Committee, with Frank serving as chairman and Waters as the third-highest Democrat in seniority. Until recently, Waters's husband, Sidney Williams, was a director of the bank. Representative Waters at one time had investments in the bank and her husband also owned stock in the firm. In addition, bank executives donated to Waters's political campaigns.

She acknowledged calling the Treasury Department on OneUnited's behalf. The bank eventually received $12 million in TARP funds. The money made its way to the bank through a special provision written into the bailout legislation. *Wall Street Journal* reporter Susan Schmidt explained, "A provision designed to aid OneUnited was written into the federal bailout legislation by Mr. Frank, who is chairman of the financial services panel. Mr. Frank said he inserted the provision to help the only African-American owned bank in his home state."

Financial regulators were not impressed with many of the bank's practices and the bank was ordered to name a new independent board. In addition, "the bank was ordered to stop paying for a Porsche used by one of its executives and its chairman's $6.4 million beachfront home in Pacific Palisades."

Measuring Political Influence

Empirical evidence also shows a systematic political component to the distribution of TARP funds. [R.] Duchin and [D.] Sosyura (2009) examined the Capital Purchase Program, the largest TARP initiative in terms of the amount of expended capital. They measured political influence by examining the number of seats held by bank executives on the board of directors at Federal Reserve banks or branches, whether the bank's headquarters was located in the district of a U.S. House member serving on a key congressional committee or subcommittee dealing with the financial service sector, the bank's lobbying expenditures, and the bank's campaign contributions to congressional candidates.

Controlling for nonpolitical bank characteristics thought to influence the distribution of TARP funds, Duchin and Sosyura found that employing a bank executive that also serves at a Federal Reserve bank was associated with a 31 percent increase in the likelihood of receiving TARP funds. Having the bank's headquarters located in the district of a U.S. Representative serving on a key financial service committee improved the chances of TARP funding by 26 percent. In addition, TARP funds flowed to those institutions that spent large sums of money lobbying and made significant contributions to politicians.

Instead of allocating funds in an effort to bring about economic recovery, legislators distributed dollars to politically connected banks.

Duchin and Sosyurn also found that political influence was strongest for poorly performing banks. Thus, political ties shifted funds to weaker institutions, a result at odds with the original stated purpose of TARP. The public, like Representative Thornberry, should be uncomfortable with the expanded role of the state. Instead of allocating funds in an effort to bring about economic recovery, legislators distributed dollars to politically connected banks.

Our focus is on the original bailout vote of each legislator. We seek to determine to what extent political considerations drove the decision by legislators to support or reject TARP.

Looking at the Political Evidence

Lawmakers made it clear that they faced a complex bill that grappled with extremely difficult issues. They assured the public that much time and effort had gone into assessing the merits of the proposed legislation. Issues such as fairness and equity, banking regulation, executive pay, and job losses all entered into their calculation. In addition, moral hazard, 401(k) values, and the proper role of the state made the vote difficult at best. But it turns out that when one moves beyond the speeches, the underlying motivation behind most votes cast was hardly complex and actually quite simple.

An examination of the bailout vote reveals that almost three-fourths of the variation in the vote from politician to politician is explained by only four variables in the House of Representatives and only five variables in the Senate. The model investigating the House vote included the following independent variables: party affiliation, tenure, membership on the Financial Services Committee, and recent contributions to each politician from the financial-services sector. In the Senate model the same variables were included with the exception that the House Committee is replaced with a Senate Committee—membership on the Banking and Urban Affairs Committee. Also, a new variable is added—the number of years until each senator faces the voters in the next election.

The dependent variable in the model is the vote—a yea or a nay—and thus, a Logit model[1] is estimated. The first bill was defeated in the House with 228 members voting against the measure and 205 voting in favor. Democrats offered the most support with 140 voting in favor and 95 voting against the legislation. Only 65 Republicans supported the bill while 133 opposed. In the Senate, the measure passed with 74 members favoring the bill and 25 against.

Campaign contributions to politicians from the financial service industry covering the years from 2003 through 2008 is used in the analysis. The industry includes security brokers and investment companies; commercial banks and bank holding companies; credit unions; finance, insurance, and real estate businesses; private equity and investment firms; banks and lending institutions; credit agencies and finance compa-

---

1. In statistics, a Logit model is used for predicting the outcome of two dependent variables with only two possible outcomes, here a yes or no vote.

nies; stock exchanges; commodity brokers/dealers; venture capital funds; securities, commodities, and investment firms; and hedge funds. . . .

Party affiliation, tenure, and contributions from the financial services sector are all significant at the 1 percent level. Specifically, the House model indicates that if members are Democrats, served for a longer period of time, or received contributions from the financial service sector, they were more likely to vote for the bill. Committee assignments are insignificant in the model.

An investigation of the Senate bailout vote analysis yields results that are similar to the House of Representatives but not identical. Again, we find that the committee assignments included in the model did not offer any explanatory power. Likewise, party affiliation and years until the next election are not significantly related to the vote. Senators with greater years of service were more likely to support the measure (at the 10 percent level of statistical significance). Contributions were associated with a vote in favor of the bailout package and this variable was significant at the 1 percent level.

Those politicians that had received greater contributions from the financial service industry were the same politicians more likely to vote for the [Wall Street] wealth transfer.

In the end, as the results make clear, the vote had very little to do with representing those on Main Street. Instead, politicians were guided by political considerations. In the House of Representatives, the longer politicians had served (safe seat), the more likely they were to vote in favor of the bill. Also, Democrats in the House were more likely to support the measure. In the Senate, party did not play a role but tenure was significantly and positively related to a yes vote.

The most interesting factor in the model is the level of campaign contributions from the financial service sector. With the public paying unprecedented attention to the decision, those politicians that had received greater contributions from the financial service industry were the same politicians more likely to vote for the wealth transfer. Wall Street, like other special interest groups in America, continues to exert an inordinate amount of influence on Congress—and Main Street, as usual, picks up the tab.

8

The Big Bank Model Must Change to Avoid Future Bailouts

Mitchell Schnurman

Mitchell Schnurman writes on business issues for the Fort Worth Star-Telegram.

The too-big-to-fail big bank model that rewards risky financial practices must change to prevent future financial bailouts. Because big banks have such an impact on the economy, these institutions know that the federal government will bail them out and thus they have no reason not to return to risky practices that threaten the economy. Unlike smaller banks that focus on relationships with their customers, big banks instead focus on transactions, paying enormous bonuses for performance, in turn encouraging risky but high profit financial practices. In this way the big bank model creates the wrong incentives. Policymakers should therefore revise this model before these risky practices lead to another economic crisis.

No one should be surprised that Wall Street is paying big bonuses, and that politicians and people are outraged about it. But who expected the banks to pull off such a fast turnaround?

Most corporate recoveries are years in the making. General Motors' revival, if it comes at all, will be a long slog. But some banks that took taxpayer money—and paid it back with interest—are world-beaters again.

A year ago, the big banks were supposedly staring into the abyss Lehman Bros [a large financial investment bank] had failed, credit markets seized up, and a global financial meltdown was looming. Central bankers jumped into action, and the U.S. government approved a $700 billion bailout.

Well, it worked. The economy stabilized, and despite the pain of double-digit unemployment, the banks are raking it in again.

Goldman Sachs posted its biggest profit ever in 2009— $13.4 billion, almost six times larger than the year before. Wells Fargo's bottom line followed the same arc, rising almost fivefold. JP Morgan Chase doubled its profit, after a $12 billion increase in interest income.

Small businesses may complain that loans are harder to get, and consumers are angry about rising credit card rates. But after the easy-credit era created a giant debt bubble, it's only natural that lending standards get tougher.

Banks are benefiting from less competition today. A number of big players were crumbling as the markets collapsed in 2008 and had to be acquired, often with a government push. Merrill Lynch, Bear Stearns, Countrywide Mortgage, Wachovia and Washington Mutual are now parts of larger banks.

If [the big banks'] rapid improvement marks a return to the old days, watch out.

Big banks also have a major stake in the stock and bond markets, which had a roaring 2009. Goldman, for instance, reported $23 billion from fixed income, currency and commodity trading, compared with less than $4 billion in 2008.

"Banks still have a lot of leverage, and that amplifies their returns," said Thomas Moeller, who teaches finance at Texas Christian University. "When times are good, they're really good."

Why Banks Were Reckless

Strong banks are vital to a recovery, so we should root for their success and hope they're a leading indicator for the rest of the economy. But if their rapid improvement marks a return to the old days, watch out.

Big banks got into trouble by betting on mortgage-backed securities, derivatives and other exotic instruments. When the investments went bad, the feds had to ride to the rescue, because some banks were deemed "too big to fail."

In essence, they could play aggressively, even recklessly, because they had a federal safety net.

"They're playing government blackjack," C.R. "Rusty" Cloutier, chief executive of Midsouth Bank in Lafayette, La., told me. "The government puts up the bet, and the banks pocket the money if they win."

Cloutier went to Washington recently to testify to a panel investigating the financial crisis. He represented community bankers and said that smaller banks focused on relationships, rather than transactions.

"We know our customers and operate under the quaint but effective practice of only lending money to people who can pay it back," he told the panel.

Wall Street is a pay-for-performance culture, and big bonuses follow rising profits. But the widespread criticism has had an effect. Goldman, for one, said it will donate $500 million from its bonus pool to charity. It's still paying each employee an average of nearly $500,000, a 46 percent increase.

A federal pay czar caps compensation at companies that still have taxpayer money. But those rules affect only a sliver of workers—about 75 out of 663,000 at three Wall Street firms, said John Benson of the Web site, efinancialcareers.com.

Bonuses are not inherently bad, not unless they create the wrong incentives.

"Most bonuses are based on growth, not long-term performance, so that's what banks got," said Scott MacDonald, who teaches banking at Southern Methodist University.

One way or another, the [big bank] model has to change, and before people forget how we got into this mess in the first place.

A Push for Reform

Last week, President Barack Obama renewed his push to reform the financial services industry. He wants to bar banks from operating hedge funds and proprietary trading if their deposits are backed by taxpayers. And he wants to strengthen liquidity requirements and oversight, so one bank's failure won't threaten the entire economy.

"Never again will the American taxpayer be held hostage by a bank that is too big to fail," Obama said.

He also took a shot at companies returning to their "old practices" and reporting "soaring profits and obscene bonuses."

"The American people have paid a very high price," Obama said. "We simply cannot return to business as usual."

To Cloutier, the community banker, the answer is to break up the banks. Reduce them to maybe one-quarter of their current size, and he says much of the risky behavior will go away. If not, the bad bets will wash out without requiring a federal rescue.

It's good news that big banks are making big profits, because they're crucial to a broader recovery. It's even comforting to be arguing about bonuses again, because they're cheaper than bailouts.

But one way or another, the model has to change, and before people forget how we got into the mess in the first place.

9

Sound Big Bank Business Practices Explain the Financial Bailout's Success

Daniel Indiviglio

Daniel Indiviglio, an associate editor at The Atlantic *from 2009 through 2011, is now Washington, D.C. columnist for* Reuters Breakingviews.

Big bank business practices did not cause the financial crisis, which is why the bank bailouts worked. Uncertainty propelled the financial crisis when stock market investors and traders learned that some large investment banks held risky assets. However, most big banks actually held few of these "toxic" securities such as mortgages given to people with poor credit. The bailout calmed this uncertainty and stabilized the market, which restored confidence. The fact that not all bailouts worked is evidence that those banks that survived with the help of bailouts did so because of sound banking practices.

In 2008, the government took historic measures to stabilize the financial industry by providing the Treasury unprecedented power to bail out the banks. Almost immediately after, the controversial move was despised by free-marketers everywhere. However, more pragmatic economic observers noted that they were unsavory, but unavoidable. 18 months later—surprise!—they actually appear to have worked pretty well.

Andrew Ross Sorkin notes this revelation in his *New York Times* column today, [April 13, 2010]. Considering the underlying causes of the financial crisis, this should not be a shock.

Stabilizing the Market

The first important objective of the bailout was to stabilize the financial markets. That happened relatively quickly. It should have: when the U.S. government makes a choice to essentially prevent an industry from failing that goes a long way in calming markets. As soon as investors realized that the risk they feared would be covered by Uncle Sam, there was far less fear about banking. The credit crunch then began to lessen.

Several months later, the government decided to conduct a series of stress tests on the largest banks. That confirmed to the market that the Treasury would stand behind these firms. Again, investors were relieved and less worried about risk. The stress tests, thus, made it even less likely the bailouts would fail.

The big banks that were given [bailout] money have largely survived because they didn't have flagrant business strategy flaws that would limit their future profitability.

The Causes of the Crisis

Uncertainty drove the credit crunch. Investors and traders suddenly realized they didn't fully understand some of the securities they owned, many of which relied on a troubled housing market. They also didn't know how big the losses were that would hit banks that also held these bad assets.

But most banks had limited exposures to these toxic securities and the broader mortgage market. Home prices can only fall so far, so the losses slowed. When the credit crunch hit its climax, many of these assets had to be marked to prices that already reflected very serious loss levels. So some of the bank losses were unrealized at the time they were taken. That would provide banks some cushion going forward and even cause some institutions to see gains if losses turned out to be lower than anticipated.

So once investors got comfortable with the banks again, and the housing market's bleeding slowed from a hemorrhage to a drip, they got much better. There was no systematic problem in their business models; they just made some really poor assumptions about what would happen in the real estate market. Once that mistake was in their past, they could go back to business as usual.

Not All Bailouts Worked—Yet

It should be noted, however, that not all of the bailouts worked, yet. The big banks that were given money have largely survived, because they didn't have flagrant business strategy flaws that would limit their future profitability. Firms that the U.S. may lose money on, including Fannie, Freddie[1] and the auto companies, are a different story. There, problems were driven by their business models. Consequently, those bailouts could ultimately fail, unless reorganization strategies work extraordinarily well and these companies manage to pay back the government over an extended time period.

Just because the bank bailout worked doesn't mean bailouts, in general, are harmless. One statistic that's hard to track is the damage caused to smaller banks by the government's implicit guarantee of the bigger ones. Even though the bailout succeeded in stabilizing the economy, government support of private firms does have significant negative consequences. That's why reform is so important to minimize the need for such bailouts in the future.

---

1. Fannie Mae is the Federal National Mortgage Association and Freddie Mac is the Federal Home Loan Mortgage Corporation.

10

Shadow Banking Practices Must Be Regulated to Prevent Future Crises

Stephen Spruiell and Kevin D. Williamson

Stephen Spruiell is a National Review Online *staff reporter and Kevin D. Williamson is a deputy managing editor of* National Review, *a conservative news magazine.*

No American with money in a traditional bank regulated by the Federal Deposit Insurance Corporation (FDIC) lost any money during the recent financial crisis. Indeed, it was the unregulated shadow banking system—financial institutions that trade in riskier financial instruments—that required a government bail-out. To prevent future bank bailouts, an FDIC-like agency should oversee this shadow banking system. The agency should be independent of the government and funded by the financial institutions it regulates. Large investment banks should maintain plans for a pre-packaged bankruptcy so that creditors are aware of the risks, which would in turn reduce particularly risky practices. Lawmakers should create well-defined rules and standards to govern these financial institutions to avoid the current improvisational approach to the financial crises.

What was so bad about the bailouts? Everything, except that they sort of worked, at least as a short-term patch-up and a bid for time. But that time is running out, and

Stephen Spruiell and Kevin D. Williamson, "Resolve to Reform: How to Get Un-TARPed and Police the Shadow Banking System," *National Review*, v. 62, no. 6, April 5, 2010. All rights reserved. Reproduced with permission.

we should now start thinking about the next crisis, and the next—and how to mitigate what cannot be avoided in the post-TARP [Troubled Asset Relief Program] era.

An Adhocracy

The really offensive thing about the bailouts was the prevailing sense of adhocracy—that Congress and the White House and the Treasury and the Fed [Federal Reserve] were more or less making things up as they went along. This bank got rescued, that one didn't. This firm got a bailout on generous terms, that one got the pillory. Dick Fuld[1] got vilified, Tim Geithner[2] got made Treasury secretary.

We need an FDIC-style resolution authority that can do for the shadow banking systems what the FDIC does for banks—police safety and soundness.

It didn't have to be that way: We have a pretty good system for regulating traditional banks and, when necessary, for taking over failed banks and "resolving" them—taking care of depositors and sorting out losses among creditors and shareholders. The Federal Deposit Insurance Corporation [FDIC] is one of the few players in the recent crisis that have acquitted themselves reasonably well. No American depositor lost a dime from his savings account, checks cleared, and everyone's ATM card kept working. The FDIC works as well as it does because there is not much adhocracy in its approach—terms

---

1. Fuld was CEO of the now bankrupt global financial investment firm Lehman Brothers, and was blamed for its collapse. Critics claim he encouraged Lehman to bankroll lenders across the country that were making convoluted loans to questionable borrowers. Lehman turned those loans into bonds and passed billions of dollars of toxic debt on to investors. Fuld received nearly $500 million in compensation during his tenure as CEO, which ended when Lehman did.
2. Geithner was president of the New York Federal Reserve Bank at the time of the financial collapse and rose to prominence early in 2009 as a key official in the government's financial rescue measures.

and practices are defined in advance, and its operations are prefunded through insurance premiums charged to the banks whose deposits it insures.

Policing the Shadow Banking System

But we also have a shadow banking system: a menagerie of hedge funds, structured-investment vehicles, non-depository investment banks, and other intermediaries that shuffle money between borrowers, lenders, and investors outside of traditional banks. Before we can get our economy fully un-TARPed ... we need an FDIC-style resolution authority that can do for the shadow banking system what the FDIC does for banks: police safety and soundness and, when necessary, take troubled institutions into custody and disassemble them in an orderly manner.

Some free-marketers will protest that such a resolution authority promises to be just another failed federal regulator, that we should "let markets work." But the bailouts have proved beyond any doubt that "too big to fail" is a durable feature of Washington's thinking about finance—the reality is that an immaculate free-market solution is not in the works. It's rather a question of what sort of regulation we are going to have and who is going to be doing it. We don't expect the new resolution authority to be perfect, but if its powers are well defined and reasonably insulated from electoral politics, it could prove as useful as the FDIC at stemming panic and containing spillovers into the real economy.

The new authority probably should be under the jurisdiction of the Federal Reserve, though its activities and the Fed's traditional monetary-policy functions should be walled off from each other. Why the Fed? It has a great deal of financial expertise and knowledge at its disposal, and it is not headed by a cabinet secretary with an eye on the next election. The Fed's haughty independence, for many a source of irritation and suspicion, is in fact its great virtue. It has made its mistakes—keeping interest rates too low for too long, and thereby helping to inflate the housing bubble—but an obsession with short-term politics is not one of them. The FDIC has enough to do, and neither Treasury nor Commerce nor any other cabinet agency should be trusted with the broad powers that any effective resolution authority would have to command.

Every TBTFI—Too Big to Fail Institution—coming under the [proposed regulatory] agency's jurisdiction [should] be required to establish and maintain, in advance, its own resolution plan.

A Pre-Packaged Bankruptcy

The institutions that make up the shadow banking system are a diverse and complicated lot: If traditional banking is a game of checkers, this is 3-D chess on dozens of boards at the same time. It is therefore likely that the regulators will lack the expertise to establish appropriate, timely resolution programs for the complex institutions they are expected to govern. The solution to that problem is found in Columbia finance professor Charles Calomiris's proposal that every TBTFI—Too Big to Fail Institution—coming under the new agency's jurisdiction be required to establish and maintain, in advance, its own resolution plan, which would be subject to regulatory approval.

Such a plan—basically, a pre-packaged bankruptcy—would make public detailed information about the distribution of losses in the event of an institutional failure—in other words, who would take how much of a haircut if the bank or fund were to find itself in dire straits. This would be a substantial improvement on the political favor-jockeying that marked the government's intervention in General Motors, for instance, or the political limbo that saw Lehman [Brothers, a large financial investment firm that collapsed in 2008] doing nothing to save itself while waiting to be rescued by a Washington bailout that never came. The authority's main job would be to keep up with the resolution plans and, when necessary, to execute them.

Like the FDIC, the new resolution authority should be prefunded, its day-to-day operations and its trust fund underwritten by insurance premiums charged to the institutions it oversees. This in itself might have a useful dampening effect: Institutions not wishing to fall under the resolution authority's jurisdiction, thereby becoming subject to the expenses and inconvenience associated with it, would have an incentive to moderate the size and complexity of their operations, which would be a good thing in many cases. Unlike TARP, the authority's trust fund should be treated as what it is—capital backing an insurance program—and restricted by statute from being used as a political slush fund. Being funded by the financial institutions themselves, it would not be subject to the whims of congressional appropriators.

Rules, processes, and standards [should] be well defined in advance—before the next crisis, and the next opportunity for the ad hoc shenanigans that made TARP the hate totem it is.

Enacting Useful Reforms

Taking a fresh regulatory approach would give us the opportunity to enact some useful reforms at the same time. At present, capital requirements—the amount of equity and other assets financial firms are required to hold in proportion to their lending—are static: X cents in capital for every $1 in, for example, regular mortgage loans. This makes them "procyclical," meaning that, during booms, banks suddenly find themselves awash in capital as their share prices and the value of their assets climb, with the effect that they can secure a lot more loans with the assets they already have on the books. But the requirements are pro-cyclical on the downside, too: During recessions, declining share and asset prices erode banks' capital base, hamstringing their operations and making financial contractions even worse. Instead, we should use counter-cyclical capital requirements: During booms, the amount of capital required to back each dollar in lending should increase on a pre-defined schedule, helping to put the brake on financial bubbles and to tamp down irrational exuberance. During downturns, capital requirements should be loosened on a predefined schedule, to facilitate lending and to keep banks from going into capital crises for mere accounting reasons. But these counter-cyclical capital requirements should begin from a higher baseline: The shadow banking system exists, in no small part, to skirt traditional capital requirements, and its scanty capital cushions helped make the recent crisis much worse than it had to be.

One other aspect of the FDIC that should be incorporated into the new resolution authority: automatic triggers. The FDIC Improvement Act ensures that the agency has relatively little regulatory discretion: If a bank fails to satisfy certain standards, the FDIC is not only empowered to move in and resolve it, but required to do so. Likewise, the resolution authority should have relatively little leeway in its operations. More than the FDIC, perhaps, due to the variety and complexity of the institutions it will be expected to oversee—but not much more. What is most important is that its rules, processes, and standards be well defined in advance—before the next crisis, and the next opportunity for the ad hoc shenanigans that made TARP the hate totem it is.

Only after the new resolution authority is set up can we really untangle ourselves from TARP and the rest of the bailout regime. That is because many of the institutions still being propped up under bailout protocols are weak, and some of them probably are going to fail. . . .

Dealing with Fannie Mae and Freddie Mac

A special situation, one that probably would exceed the new authority's resources, is the sorry case of Fannie Mae [the Federal National Mortgage Association] and Freddie Mac [the Federal Home Loan Mortgage Corporation]. The government-sponsored (now government-owned) enterprises present a real obstacle to returning to a more normal economy. But the first step is relatively straightforward: The government should start by admitting that it is on the hook for all of Fannie and Freddie's losses, not just the $100 billion it has already loaned the companies. The White House still is not accounting for Fannie and Freddie the way it accounts for other federal entities. According to one estimate, Fannie and Freddie's liabilities total $6.3 trillion, every dollar of which is now the taxpayers' potential problem.

Policymakers are understandably reluctant to add such an enormous sum to the national balance sheet, but they could start by accounting for the $300 billion the Congressional Budget Office says it costs to insure the agencies' liabilities against the possibility of default over the next ten years. Adding Fannie and Freddie to budget calculations would, we hope, pressure policymakers to reduce taxpayer exposure to the GSEs [government-sponsored enterprises] by winding down their large portfolios and breaking them up—instead of doing what they are currently doing, which is close to the opposite of that.

Of course, these are our ideal reforms, and they bear only a coincidental resemblance to those that Chris Dodd and other congressional panjandrums [self-important pretentious official] are bandying about. Dodd's resolution authority would leave too much discretion to politicians to offer insolvent firms permanent life support, Fannie- and Freddie-style, rather than force them into orderly liquidation.

Other proposals we've seen emerge from Congress look more like reorganization than reform, reminding us of the man who wrote, "We tend as a nation to meet any new situation by reorganizing; and a wonderful method it can be for creating the illusion of progress while producing confusion, inefficiency, and demoralization." It is one thing when this reorganizing involves the renaming of some unimportant bureaucracy, but when it comes to financial reform, the illusion of progress is dangerous. Already it can be argued that investors' appetite for risk has returned to pre-crisis levels as government support of the banking system has bolstered the impression that there is no such thing as a bad credit risk on Wall Street. A resolution authority, properly structured, could mitigate this moral hazard by reacquainting the bankers with the prospect of failure and their creditors with the prospect of losses. Whether we will get one is another question entirely.

11

Regulation Will Not Prevent Future Bailouts

William Poole

William Poole, CEO of the Federal Reserve Bank of St. Louis from March 1998 to March 2008, is a senior fellow at the Cato Institute, a libertarian think tank, and scholar in residence at the University of Delaware, Newark. The following viewpoint is taken from a speech delivered at the Chartered Financial Analyst Institute in April 2009.

Regulation is an inadequate way to prevent future bank bailouts. Government-run agencies are too vulnerable to influence and regulation puts some financial institutions at a competitive advantage. The best way to prevent another bailout is to allow free market principles to discourage risky practices. For example, the bank's creditors must be at risk to discourage uncertain strategies. In addition, removing the tax break on interest would discourage businesses from getting too deeply into debt. Large financial investment banks must also be required to maintain more subordinated long-term debt, which in bankruptcy has a lower priority for payment. This policy would create a cushion against losses and force large financial institutions to convince creditors and the market that they are strong.

In an interview in March 2009, U.S. Treasury secretary Timothy Geithner stated:

> People across the country are angry and frustrated, as they should be, that this economy, the United States of America,

Abridged version of William Poole, "Moral Hazard: The Long-Lasting Legacy of Bailouts," *Financial Analysts Journal*, v. 65, no. 6, November/December 2009. All rights reserved. Reproduced with permission.

got itself in the position where enormous damage has been done as a consequence of a long period of excess risk-taking without meaningful adult supervision.

And the consequences of that are tragic because they're basically fundamentally unfair; because people who were careful and responsible, conservative in their decisions, are suffering a lot from the consequences of mistakes they were not part of.

Washington is not the place to make decisions on details of how to run businesses, whether or not they are receiving federal support.

Stronger language than Secretary Geithner's is appropriate: The bailout regime in which we find ourselves is an affront to the market and an affront to democracy. These affronts will continue to affect policy by making many companies skittish about the prospect of federal intervention in their management, especially about issues of corporate compensation. The U.S. government—the U.S. Treasury and the Fed [Federal Reserve] together—must devise an exit strategy for a way out of the current environment, in which many large companies are too big to fail. Unfortunately, the federal government has offered no vision of a genuinely reformed financial structure. The government's vision seems to be more of the same, with a heavier dose of "tougher" regulation but without much specificity as to what that means.

Public outrage over bonuses and corporate perks is unfortunate—Washington is not the place to make decisions on details of how to run businesses, whether or not they are receiving federal support. The outrage, however, is fully justified at a deeper level. That no satisfactory plan has emerged as of this writing, some 20 months after the Bear Stearns [a global investment bank] bailout, is incomprehensible. Now, all large banks are backstopped by the federal government; and should any other large firm run into trouble, it too would likely receive federal support.

Nearly everyone agrees that the bailout regime must not be allowed to persist. But I differ profoundly with Secretary Geithner's implication that what is needed is more regulation—"meaningful adult supervision," as he puts it. Regulation itself cannot be the solution because if regulators make mistakes—as they do and will—the government is once again likely to bail out banks deemed too big to fail.

Allowing the Market to Mitigate Risk

The problem is simple to state. The only resolutional procedure that will control moral hazard is one in which some creditors will take a hit if a large firm fails. Wiping out shareholders is not enough—creditors of these highly leveraged firms must be at risk. I see no imminent prospect that the federal government, including the Fed, would allow a large firm to fail with losses to creditors. Some brave talk is heard about forcing creditors to take losses, but when faced with the actual possibility, what will likely control the outcome is fear of another financial meltdown, such as the one that followed the failure of Lehman Brothers [a large financial investment bank].

Regulators sometimes abuse their power or act in ways that do not reflect market realities.

We need to look at the situation in a different way, by focusing on designing incentives that enable market forces to lead firms, or force them, to pursue less risky strategies. The proposal outlined in this article changes incentives in fundamental ways; it encourages a different way of thinking about fixing our financial services industry. . . .

The Influence of Lobbyists

The question is whether regulators can enforce constraints on firms that are robust with respect to surprise events. For a number of reasons, the answer is no.

In our democracy, one issue is that the U.S. Congress inevitably affects the regulatory process. . . . Regulation will not be left to technocrats, nor should it be. Regulators sometimes abuse their power or act in ways that do not reflect market realities. Congress ought to intervene to control regulatory abuses. The question of what is an abuse and what is not is ultimately a political issue.

We can certainly expect that companies will continue to lobby to affect regulatory rules and outcomes. As early as the late 1960s, economists understood risks to the savings and loan (S&L) industry, but that industry, homebuilders, mortgage finance companies, and congressional advocates of expanded home ownership prevailed to maintain weak regulation in the 1970s and to weaken it further in the early 1980s. In this episode, which ultimately cost taxpayers about $150 billion, economists and regulators did not miss the boat but were unable to prevail.

As another example, long before the huge increase in the issuance of subprime mortgages, former Fed chairman Alan Greenspan warned repeatedly of dangers in the structure and regulation of Fannie Mae (Federal National Mortgage Association) and Freddie Mac (Federal Home Loan Mortgage Corporation). Starting in 2002, I gave a number of speeches on the same theme. Vigorous lobbying and large campaign contributions by these government-sponsored enterprises and their executives—and the failure of Congress to understand the risks—prevented reform. The federal government took over Fannie Mae and Freddie Mac in September 2008, and the cost to taxpayers will be in the hundreds of billions of dollars. Worse yet, congressional supporters of Fannie Mae and Freddie Mac—those responsible for preventing reform—appear to have dodged voters' ire. Anyone who believes that we can escape similar situations in the future does not understand how democracy works.

Practices That Reduce Competition

We live in an intensely competitive global environment. If regulations put particular types of firms at a competitive disadvantage, other firms that are able to sidestep regulations will offer financial services and take business away from regulated firms. Some firms operating in U.S. markets have charters from foreign countries, and international agreement on regulatory standards may be impossible. Aggressive firms will use their national governments to further their commercial interests. And even if our current financial crisis leads to international regulatory standards, the innovative environment in which we live will soon make those standards obsolete in certain respects.

> *The present regulatory authority over banks did not prevent the crisis or lead to the closures of any large banks.*

Given the thriving legal practice in regulatory compliance and in the closely related field of regulatory avoidance, to expect that such practices will disappear or can be so controlled by Congress that lawyers and accountants will never again find or create regulatory loopholes is a pipe dream. In time, the current financial crisis will fade into history. Whatever restraints we may observe over the next few years will disappear, and we will be back to business as usual. . . .

Creating new regulatory authority over large firms . . . simply does not address the main problem. The present regulatory authority over banks did not prevent the crisis or lead to the closure of any large banks. Lehman Brothers, a large investment bank, was allowed to fail, but no large commercial banks have yet failed. They have all been bailed out, even though the regulators have all the authority they need to close a big bank. Recognizing the necessity of keeping the big banks afloat during the current financial crisis does nothing to preclude similar decisions in the future.

A Reform Plan

Instead of more regulators with more power, we need to change the incentives under which firms operate. Our firms got into trouble because they had too much leverage and too much of their debt was short term. They were subject to too little market discipline. Finally, we need a market-based method for forcing large firms to scale back their operations in an orderly way when they get into trouble. These issues can be addressed by changing the incentives under which firms operate.

Four problems must be solved. First, many firms have too little capital relative to the risks they run. Unfortunately, capital inadequacy is often revealed only after the fact. We need arrangements that force banks to hold more capital than might seem necessary. Second, banks need long-maturity capital that cannot run. Third, we need to rely more on market discipline to deny funds to banks deemed risky. Fourth, when a bank needs to be restructured, the bank, rather than the federal government, should manage the restructuring.

Eliminating Tax Breaks

A straightforward fix for excessive leverage can be achieved through the tax system. Companies borrow, in part, because they believe that debt capital is cheaper than equity capital. That is certainly the case under the U.S. corporate tax system because interest is a deductible business expense in calculating income subject to tax, whereas dividends are not deductible. A useful reform would be to eliminate the deductibility of interest on business and personal tax returns. A quick look at 2006 data, the latest available in the U.S. Internal Revenue Service

Statistics of Income, indicates that for the corporate sector as a whole, eliminating the deductibility of interest would more than double corporate income subject to tax. Cutting the statutory corporate tax rate to 15 percent would have left revenues from the corporate tax system more or less unchanged in 2006. Given the current and prospective economic situation, the corporate profits tax would have to be cut further for revenue neutrality in the near term, perhaps to 10 percent.

To smooth the transition, interest deductibility could be phased out over the next 10 years. Next year, 90 percent of interest would be deductible; the following year, 80 percent would be deductible, and so forth, until interest would no longer be deductible at all. The same reform would apply to all business entities; partnerships, for example, should not be able to deduct interest if corporations cannot.

With this simple change, the federal government would encourage businesses and households to become less leveraged. We have learned that leverage makes not only individual companies more vulnerable to failure but also the economy less stable. We use tax laws all the time to promote socially desirable behavior; eliminating the deductibility of interest would reduce the risk of failure of large companies—especially, large firms—and thereby reduce the collateral damage inflicted by such failures.

Maintaining Long-Term Debt Capital

A lesson from our current financial crisis—not a new lesson but an old one—is that firms can collapse suddenly, in part because too much of their debt has very short maturities. An idea favored by economists for many years is to require banks to maintain a substantial block of subordinated, long-term debt in their capital structure.

To illustrate, the following proposal would apply to every firm with a bank charter, including savings institutions and credit unions, above some threshold, such as total assets greatest than $50 billion. Every such bank would have to issue subordinated debt equal to 10 percent of its total liabilities. The debt would consist of 10-year uncollateralized notes that were subordinated to all other debt obligations of the bank. With 10-year notes equal to 10 percent of the bank's total liabilities, the bank would have to refinance one-tenth of its subordinated debt every year, equal to 1 percent of its total liabilities. The subordinated debt would be in addition to existing requirements for equity capital.

Subordinated debt has several important advantages. We have seen that banks do not have an adequate cushion against losses under current capital requirements. If taxpayers are to be expected to stand behind our giant banks, they deserve a larger cushion against the banks' mistakes. More importantly, because banks would have to go to the market every year to sell new subordinated debt, they would have to convince the market that they are safe. A bank that found selling new subordinated debt too expensive would have to shrink by 10 percent. Restructuring a bank at an annual rate of 10 percent is perfectly feasible, and the restructuring would be managed by the bank and not by the government.

A subordinated debt requirement has a significant advantage over a higher equity capital requirement, which is one of the regulatory changes being discussed. A subordinated debt requirement entails much more market discipline because a bank must either go to the market every year to replace maturing debt or shrink. If a bank's prospects appear poor to investors, its stock price will decline and it may be unable to sell more equity. But it is not forced to shrink under these circumstances, nor will regulators necessarily force a bank to shrink. Market discipline through subordinated debt would be much more rigorous than any discipline regulators are likely to apply. Bankers will argue that market discipline from subordinated debt would be too rigorous and go too far in discouraging risk taking. Does anyone, however, defend the risks that banks took that created the current financial crisis? Would we not be much better off if bankers had believed that subprime mortgage paper was too risky for bank portfolios? The economy will work better if the banking sector becomes a smaller, but more stable, part of the economy.

Putting Creditors at Risk

This point deserves repetition: To control moral hazard, some creditors—not just equity owners—must be at risk. Among creditors, holders of subordinated debt are most at risk, and they provide maximum market discipline. In the event of a bank insolvency, the FDIC would seize the bank and cover insured depositors. Other creditors would be protected because losses would go first to equity and then to subordinated debt. If those forms of capital were insufficient to cover the losses, then other uninsured creditors would take a hit. A subordinated debt requirement would be a valuable reform because the debt is long term, cannot run, and puts a substantial block of creditors at risk.

Federal protection, inevitably accompanied by intrusive regulation and control, will leave a legacy of uncompetitive behavior.

These two reforms—phasing out the deductibility of interest on business tax returns and requiring banks to maintain subordinated debt in their capital structure—would change the incentives under which firms operate. Firms would be more stable, and the economy would also be more stable.

These proposals are not radical. They rely on market incentives and avoid intrusive and ultimately ineffective government regulation. If we are unwilling to approach the issue of financial stability from the perspective of getting the incentives right, then we will not enjoy financial stability in the long run.

Blunting Competition

Financial bailouts, in the form of infusions of government funds to keep companies afloat, are part of a more general phenomenon of special government support of particular companies or industries to blunt the normal forces of competition. Propping up companies is unsuccessful in the long run. Starting in the 1960s, government actions designed to assist the S&L industry stifled necessary adjustments, and most S&Ls ended up failing, at a cost to taxpayers of roughly $150 billion. The federal government should not repeat that performance.

These lessons are not confined to the financial sector. Over the years, a number of manufacturing industries have received assistance through restrictions on international trade. Companies obtain these favors, costly to consumers and taxpayers, through the political process. Sadly for the presumably protected companies and their workers, their confidence in protection leads them to delay adjustments. As the cost of protection and bailouts becomes politically untenable, the scale of assistance winds down and once-great companies decline and perhaps fail. This process is playing out today for General Motors and Chrysler. Eventually, taxpayers will tire of supporting these companies. But federal protection, inevitably accompanied by intrusive regulation and control, will leave a legacy of uncompetitive behavior. Similar protection, if long continued, will ruin our large banks as well.

In short, the federal government should design and implement an exit strategy for a way out of the current bailout regime, which would be in the best interests of both taxpayers and companies. Without a plan for an orderly adjustment, even with all the pain that adjustment brings, we have only heartbreak ahead of us.

Investors need to understand the fundamentals of reforms that work and those that fail. Reforms that change incentives in appropriate ways work, and those that rely on regulation do not. If the federal government does not offer a plan that changes the incentives under which firms operate, then we cannot expect a more stable financial future. We may muddle along, and things will look better as the economy recovers from recession. Nevertheless, without fundamental reform that moves us decisively away from the risk of further bailouts, the financial system will remain unstable. Whenever a solvency issue arises, so too will debate over a possible bailout. A bailout world is an unstable world.

12

Temporarily Nationalizing Banks Would Punish Their Risky Behavior

Joseph E. Stiglitz

Joseph E. Stiglitz, professor at Columbia University, received the Nobel Prize in Economics in 2001.

A temporary nationalization of large investment banks that employ risky banking practices is necessary to get banks back to lending. While saving these banks is necessary, rescuing the bankers that promoted the high-risk practices that led to the financial crises is not. Moreover, the bailout has not been transparent. Thus, banks did not have to account for bailout money and rather than resume lending are paying out executive bonuses and stockholder dividends. Claims that the government cannot be trusted to run banks lack credibility since the private sector obviously failed miserably. To get the economy moving, the government should nationalize "bad banks," change their behavior, and teach them to lend money prudently. When the economy improves, the government can return these banks to the private sector.

The news that even Alan Greenspan and Senator Chris Dodd[1] suggest that bank nationalization may be necessary shows how desperate the situation has become. It has been

---

1. In a note following the publication of the article, the editor explained that it had erroneously stated that Senator Christopher Dodd supports bank nationalization. According to the article editor, Dodd had in fact said that he does not welcome nationalization, but "we may end up having to do that."

obvious for some time that a government takeover of our banking system—perhaps along the lines of what Norway and Sweden did in the '90s—is the only solution. It should be done, and done quickly, before even more bailout money is wasted.

The problem with America's banks is not just one of liquidity. Years of reckless behavior, including bad lending and gambling with derivatives, have left them, in effect, bankrupt. If our government were playing by the rules—which require shutting down banks with inadequate capital—many, if not most, banks would go out of business. But because faulty accounting practices don't force banks to mark down all their assets to current market prices, they may nominally meet capital requirements—at least for a while.

American banks have polluted the global economy with toxic waste; it is a matter of equity and efficiency that they must be forced . . . to pay the price of cleaning it up.

Who Should Bear the Losses?

No one knows for sure how big the hole is; some estimates put the number at $2 trillion or $3 trillion, or more. So the question is, Who is going to bear the losses? Wall Street would like nothing better than a steady drip of taxpayer money. But the experience in other countries suggests that when financial markets run the show, the costs can be enormous. Countries like Argentina, Chile and Indonesia spent 40 percent or more of their GDP [gross domestic product] to bail out their banks. For the United States, the worry is that the $700 billion appropriated for the bank bailout may turn out to be just a small down payment.

The cost to the government is especially important, given the legacy of debt from the Bush administration, which saw the national debt soar from $5.7 trillion to more than $10 trillion. Unless care is taken, government spending on the bailout will crowd out other vital government programs, from Social Security to future investments in technology.

There is a basic principle in environmental economics called "the polluter pays": polluters must pay for the cost of cleaning up their pollution. American banks have polluted the global economy with toxic waste; it is a matter of equity and efficiency that they must be forced, now or later, to pay the price of cleaning it up. As long as the banking sector feels that it will be bailed out of disasters—even ones it created—we will continue to have a moral hazard. Only by making sure that the sector pays the costs of its actions will efficiency be restored.

The full costs of those mistakes include not just the $700 billion bailout but the almost $3 trillion shortfall between the economy's potential output and its actual output resulting from the crisis. Since we are not forcing banks to pay these full costs imposed on society, we should hear no complaints from them about paying for the much smaller direct costs of the bailout.

Any solution should make it less likely, not more likely, that we will have problems in the future.

The politicians responsible for the bailout keep saying, "We had no choice. We had a gun pointed at our heads. Without the bailout, things would have been even worse." This may or may not be true, but in any case the argument misses a critical distinction between saving the banks and saving the bankers and shareholders. We could have saved the banks but let the bankers and shareholders go. The more we leave in the pockets of the shareholders and the bankers, the more that has to come out of the taxpayers' pockets.

A Dismal Failure

There are a few basic principles that should guide our bank bailout. The plan needs to be transparent, cost the taxpayer as little as possible and focus on getting the banks to start lending again to sectors that create jobs. It goes without saying that any solution should make it less likely, not more likely, that we will have problems in the future.

By these standards, the TARP [Troubled Asset Relief Program] bailout has so far been a dismal failure. Unbelievably expensive, it has failed to rekindle lending. Former Treasury Secretary Henry Paulson gave the banks a big handout; what taxpayers got in return was worth less than two-thirds of what we gave the big banks—and the value of what we got has dropped precipitously since.

Since TARP facilitated the consolidation of banks, the problem of "too big to fail" has become worse, and therefore the excessive risk-taking that it engenders has grown worse. The banks carried on paying out dividends and bonuses and didn't even pretend to resume lending. "Make more *loans?*" John Hope III, chair of Whitney National Bank in New Orleans, said to a room full of Wall Street analysts in November. The taxpayers put out $350 billion and didn't even get the right to find out what the money was being spent on, let alone have a say in what the banks did with it.

TARP's failure comes as no surprise: incentives matter. Bankers won't restart lending unless they have a reason to do so or are forced. Receiving billions of dollars in bonus pay for racking up record losses is a peculiar "incentive" structure. Bankers have been accused of unbounded greed using hard-earned taxpayer dollars for bonuses and dividends, but economists more calmly observe: they were simply responding rationally to the incentives and constraints they faced.

Even if the banks had not poured out the money in bonuses as we were pouring it in, they might not have restarted lending; they might have just hoarded it. Recapitalization enables them to lend. But there is a difference between the ability to lend and the willingness to lend. With the economy plunging into deep recession, the risks of lending are enormous. TARP did nothing to require or create incentives for new lending, focusing instead on cleaning up past mistakes. We need to be forward-looking, reducing the risk of new lending. Just think of what new lending $700 billion could have financed. Leveraged on a modest ten-to-one basis, it could have supported $7 trillion of new lending—more than enough to meet business's requirements.

The bad bank, without nationalization, is a bad idea.

Flawed Attempts to Restart Lending

Policy-makers have been flailing around, trying to figure out how to get lending restarted. It is not hard to do—if the government bears all or most of the risk. The Federal Reserve is, in effect, making major loans to America's corporate giants, giving them a big advantage over traditional job creators, America's small- and medium-size enterprises. We have no idea if the Fed is doing a good job of assessing risk and whether interest rates commensurate with the risks are being charged. Given the Fed's recent record, there is no reason for confidence. But there is a consensus that whatever the Fed is doing, it is not enough. . . .

I believe that the bad bank, without nationalization, is a bad idea. We should reject any plan that involves "cash for trash." It is another example of the voodoo economics that has marked the financial sector—the kind of alchemy that allowed the banks to slice and dice F-rated subprime mortgages into supposedly A-rated securities. Somehow, it is believed that moving the bad assets around into an aggregator bank will create value. But I suspect that Wall Street is enthusiastic about the plan not because bankers believe that government has a comparative advantage in garbage disposal but because they hope for a nontransparent bonanza from the Treasury in the form of high prices for their junk.

If the government takes over banks that don't meet the minimum capital requirements, placing them in federal conservatorship, then these pricing problems are no longer important. Under this scenario, pricing is just an accounting entry between two pockets of the government. Whether the government finds it useful to gather all the bad assets into a bad bank is a matter of management: Norway chose not to; Sweden chose to. But Sweden wasn't foolish enough to try to buy bad assets from private banks, as many in America are advocating. It was only under government ownership of the entire bank that the bad bank was created. Norway's experience was perhaps somewhat better, but the circumstances were different. Given the complexity and scale of the mess Wall Street has gotten us into, I suspect we will want to gather the problems together, net out the derivative positions (something that will be much easier to do under conservatorship and a significant achievement in its own right, with major benefits in risk reduction) and eventually restructure and dispose of the assets. . . .

Is There an Alternative?

Firms often get into trouble—accumulating more debt than they can repay. There is a time-honored way of resolving the problem, called "financial reorganization," or bankruptcy. Bankruptcy scares many people, but it shouldn't. All that happens is that the financial claims on the firm get restructured. When the firm is in very bad trouble, the shareholders get wiped out, and the bondholders become the new shareholders. When things are less serious, some of the debt is converted into equity. In any case, without the burden of monthly debt payments, the firm can return to profitability. America is lucky in having a particularly effective way of giving firms a fresh start—Chapter 11 of our bankruptcy code, which has been used repeatedly, for example, by the airlines. Airplanes keep flying; jobs and assets are preserved. Under new management, and without the burden of debt, the airline can go on making a contribution to our society.

Banks differ in only one respect. The failure of a bank results in particular hardship to depositors and can lead to broader problems in the economy. These are among the reasons that the government has provided deposit insurance. But this means that when banks fail, the government comes in to pick up the pieces—and this is different from when the local pizza parlor fails. Worse still, long experience has taught us that when banks are at risk of failure, their managers engage in behaviors that risk losing even more taxpayer money. They may, for instance, undertake big bets: if they win, they keep the proceeds; if they lose, so what?—they would have died anyway. That's why we have laws that say when a bank's capital is low, it should be shut down. We don't wait for the till to be empty. Because the government is on the hook for so much money, it has to take an active role in managing the restructuring; even in the case of airline bankruptcy, courts typically appoint someone to oversee the restructuring to make sure that the claimants' interests are served.

Usually, the process is done smoothly. The government finds a healthy bank to take over the failed bank. To get the healthy bank to do this, it often has to "fill in the hole," making up for the difference between the value of what the bank owes depositors and the value of the bank's assets. It's no different from an ordinary takeover or merger, except the government facilitates the process. Typically, in the process, shareholders get wiped out, and often the government and/or private investors may put in additional money.

Occasionally, the government can't find a healthy bank to take over the failed bank. Then it has to take over the failed bank itself. Usually, it restructures the bank, shutting down many of the branches and lending departments with particularly bad track records. Then it sells the bank. We can call this "temporary nationalization" if we want. But whatever we call it, it's no big deal. Not surprisingly, the banks are trying to scare us into believing that it would be the end of the world as we know it. Of course, it can be done badly (Lehman Brothers, for example). But there are far more examples of it being done well. . . .

The Good Bank Proposal

Gradually America is realizing that we must do something—now. We already have a framework for dealing with banks whose capital is inadequate. We should use it, and quickly, with perhaps some modifications to take care of the unusual nature of today's problems. There are several ways we can proceed. One innovative proposal (variants of which have been floated by Willem Buiter at the London School of Economics and by [Hungarian-American businessman] George Soros) entails the creation of a Good Bank. Rather than dump the bad assets on the government, we would strip out the good assets—those that can be easily priced. If the value of claims by depositors and other claims that we decide need to be protected is less than the value of the assets, then the government would write a check to the Old Bank (we could call it the Bad Bank). If the reverse is true, then the government would have a senior claim on the Old Bank. In normal times, it would be easy to recapitalize the Good Bank privately. These are not normal times, so the government might have to run the bank for a while.

Meanwhile, the Old Bank would be left with the task of disposing of its toxic assets as best it can. Because the Old Bank's capital is inadequate, it couldn't take deposits, unless it found enough capital privately to recapitalize itself. How much shareholders and bondholders got would depend on how well management did in disposing of these assets—and how well they did in ensuring that management didn't overpay itself.

The Good Bank proposal has the advantage of avoiding the N-word: nationalization. Some believe a more polite term, "conservatorship" as it was called in the case of Fannie Mae [the Federal National Mortgage Association], may be more palatable. It should be clear, though, that whatever it is called, the Good Bank proposal entails little more than playing by longstanding rules, a variant of standard practices to deal with firms whose liabilities exceed their assets.

There is every reason to believe that a temporarily nationalized bank will behave much better ... simply because we will have changed the perverse incentives.

Those who say the government cannot be trusted to allocate capital efficiently sound unconvincing these days. After all, it's not as though the private sector did a very good job. No peacetime government has wasted resources on the scale of America's private financial system. Wall Street's incentives structures were designed to encourage shortsighted and excessively risky behavior. The bankers were supposed to understand risk, but they did not understand the most elementary principles of information asymmetry, risk correlation and fat-tailed distributions. Most of them, while they may have been ethically challenged, were really guided in their behavior by the perverse incentives they championed. The result was that they did not even serve their shareholders well; from 2004 to 2008, net profits of many of the major banks were negative.

Changing Incentives

There is every reason to believe that a temporarily nationalized bank will behave much better—even if most of the employees are still the same—simply because we will have changed the perverse incentives. Besides, a government-run bank might spend some time and money teaching its employees about risk management, good lending practices, social responsibility and ethics. The experience elsewhere, including in the Scandinavian countries, shows that the whole process can be done well—and when the economy is eventually restored to prosperity, the profitable banks can be returned to the private sector. What is required is not rocket science. Banks simply need to get back to what they were supposed to do: lending money, on a prudent basis, to businesses and households, based not just on collateral but on a good assessment of the use to which borrowers will put the money and their ability to repay it.

Meanwhile, there needs to be an orderly plan for disposing of the old bad assets. There is no magic in moving them around from one owner to another. In some countries, government agencies (often hiring private subcontractors) have done a good job of selling off the assets. Other countries (including some hit in the East Asia crisis a decade ago) have had an unfortunate experience, bringing in investment banks and hedge funds to dispose of their assets. These institutions simply held them for the short time it took the economy to recover and made a huge capital gain at the expense of the country's taxpayers. To add insult to injury, some even took advantage of tax havens to avoid paying taxes on those huge profits. These experiences suggest caution in turning to hedge funds and other investment firms.

Every downturn comes to an end. Eventually we will be able to sell the restructured banks at a good price—though, one hopes, not one based on the irrational exuberant expectation of another financial bubble. The notion that we will make a profit from the bailouts—which the financial sector tried to convince us were "investments"—seems to have dropped from public discourse. But at least we can use the proceeds of the eventual sale of the restructured banks to pay down the huge deficit that this financial debacle will have brought onto our nation.

13

The Tough Requirements of the Auto Industry Bailout Saved Many Jobs

Jonathan Cohn

Jonathan Cohn writes on public policy issues for The New Republic, *a liberal news magazine.*

Despite claims that the auto bailout was a bad idea, most of the automakers are back to making money and cars. Even some of the auto bailout's early critics concede that the program is showing promise. For example, some analysts claimed that the government would manage the automakers poorly. In truth, the Obama administration has been tough, forcing General Motors to remove top managers and file bankruptcy—in essence wiping out shareholders. The claim that the goal was to reward political favors is also unsupported. In fact, the administration sought a wide range of views, putting economic needs ahead of politics. Indeed, the bailout saved hundreds of thousands of American jobs.

General Motors made news twice this week [October 2010]. First it announced that it was investing $190 million in a Michigan factory that will build its newest Cadillac and, along the way, create 600 jobs. Then it announced it would be buying back some of the preferred stock now owned by the Treasury Department, further reducing its debt to the government.

Even after the repurchase, GM will still owe the taxpayers around $40 billion. And the new GM workers are making a lot less money than old ones do. But the news is still pretty good—and, more important, it's not isolated. The Detroit Three are making money these days and, if you believe the automotive magazines, they are making good cars, too.

Of course, you wouldn't know it from the political debate. President Obama's critics have vilified the auto industry rescue and most Americans, weary of bailouts, seem to oppose it. But I've long held a different opinion. Readers may recall my staunch defense of the auto industry and efforts to rescue it. And although I've been reluctant to revisit the subject prematurely, the signs of success are becoming impossible to ignore. You don't even have to take my word for it.

A Change of Heart

Back in the spring of 2009, when Obama was debating what to do with the car companies, the *Economist* magazine came out hard against a rescue. It's about what you'd expect from a publication that extols the virtues of the free market so consistently and without qualification. And it's why their subsequent change of heart, published a few weeks ago, is worth taking so seriously:

> Many people thought this bail-out (and a smaller one involving Chrysler, an even sicker firm) unwise. Governments have historically been lousy stewards of industry. Lovers of free markets (including *The Economist*) feared that Mr Obama might use GM as a political tool: perhaps favouring the unions who donate to Democrats or forcing the firm to build smaller, greener cars than consumers want to buy. The label "Government Motors" quickly stuck, evoking images of clunky committee-built cars that burned banknotes instead of petrol—all run by what Sarah Palin might call the socialist-in-chief.
>
> Yet the doomsayers were wrong. . . . Mr Obama has been tough from the start. GM had to promise to slim down dra-

matically—cutting jobs, shuttering factories and shedding brands—to win its lifeline. The firm was forced to declare bankruptcy. Shareholders were wiped out. Top managers were swept aside. Unions did win some special favours: when Chrysler was divided among its creditors, for example, a union health fund did far better than secured bondholders whose claims should have been senior. Congress has put pressure on GM to build new models in America rather than Asia, and to keep open dealerships in certain electoral districts. But by and large Mr Obama has not used his stakes in GM and Chrysler for political ends. On the contrary, his goal has been to restore both firms to health and then get out as quickly as possible. GM is now profitable again and Chrysler, managed by Fiat, is making progress. Taxpayers might even turn a profit when GM is sold.

[The auto bailout] prevented a massive, concentrated unemployment hit when the economy could ill afford it.

Getting Something in Return

Megan McArdle, who writes for the *Atlantic*, was equally critical of the rescue. And, like the editors of the *Economist*, her policy instincts are strongly libertarian. But after visiting Detroit she, too, has revised her opinion. Although she stops well short of pronouncing it a success, she agrees it hasn't been a boondoggle:

> Post-bankruptcy, GM is unquestionably a more viable firm than the stumbling giant we put on life support two years ago. The worst fears of many critics—including me—were overblown. The government did not simply leave the bloated legacy costs intact in order to protect its political friends. . . .
>
> The bailout wasn't a good idea, and it will probably cost billions. But the government wastes billions of dollars every year, because for the United States, $1 billion adds up to the equivalent of less than one venti latte per American. At least

in this case, we got something in return: a functional car company, resurrected from the ashes of the old GM's bloated carcass. Americans probably won't notice the few extra dollars they spent on the bailout. But they may eventually be glad when another shiny new Buick Enclave rolls off the Lansing assembly line, and into their driveway.

Give credit to McArdle and to the editors of the *Economist*: Faced with contravening facts, they've modified their assessments. (Let the record show my judgment was off, too: I had thought even a structured bankruptcy might cripple sales. Quite obviously, it did not.) I'm more sanguine about the return on the government's investment than McArdle; remember, it prevented a massive, concentrated unemployment hit when the economy could ill afford it. But I would agree much could still go wrong. GM still has a huge, unfunded pension obligation; friends with ties to the company tell me that it still has too much middle management. Chrysler's situation raises more questions.

[President Barack Obama can] point to the tens of thousands of jobs—actually, make that hundreds of thousands of jobs—that didn't disappear.

Putting Policy Before Politics

But McArdle and the *Economist* editors want to make sure nobody takes from this episode the lesson that government can reliably manage an enterprise like the auto bailout. There we part company more clearly. This success, however partial and tentative, isn't accidental. It's a product of hard work by public officials who wanted to do right by their citizens. As Steven Rattner details in *Overhaul*, Obama and his advisers conducted extensive analysis and entertained a wide-ranging internal debate, putting policy well before politics.

I'm not saying they got everything right—not on this issue and not, for that matter, on many others. But they performed the same due diligence we expect of the private sector but have been told, by generations of conservatives, we can't expect of the government. Maybe it's time we revisited those expectations.

Still, designing policy is one thing. Selling it is quite another. Americans on the whole thought the bailout was too generous; those whose livelihoods depend on the auto industry thought it wasn't generous enough. Notwithstanding the announcements of new plants and new jobs, Obama can't point to the tens of thousands of new, high-paying jobs he created. All he can do is point to the tens of thousands of jobs—actually, make that hundreds of thousands of jobs— that didn't disappear. Things are a lot better, but they aren't good. And that's not a great slogan.

Making cars? Yeah, administration can do that. The problem is the bumper stickers.

14

The Long-Term Costs of the Auto Industry Bailout Are Significant

David Skeel

David Skeel, a professor of law at the University of Pennsylvania, is the author of The New Financial Deal: Understanding the Dodd-Frank Act and Its (Unintended) Consequences.

Although the government considers the auto bailout a success, the long-term costs will be significant. Moreover, the bailout was not necessary, as a standard bankruptcy could have successfully restructured the automakers. The bailout was politically motivated, favoring unions and specific creditors. Thus, bids to take over the automakers were a sham, as the government only considered those bids that included these favors. In addition, the reported costs of the bailout do not count the loss of tax revenue when the automakers deduct their losses nor the indirect cost of sending the message that if a politically important industry is at risk, the government will come to its rescue.

President Obama's visit to a Chrysler plant in Toledo, Ohio, on Friday [June 3, 2011] was the culmination of a campaign to portray the auto bailouts as a brilliant success with no unpleasant side effects. "The industry is back on its feet," the president said, "repaying its debt, gaining ground."

If the government hadn't stepped in and dictated the terms of the restructuring, the story goes, General Motors and

Chrysler would have collapsed, and at least a million jobs would have been lost. The bailouts averted disaster, and they did so at remarkably little cost.

The long-term costs of the [auto] bailouts will be enormous.

Enormous Long-Term Costs

The problem with this happy story is that neither of its parts is accurate. Commandeering the bankruptcy process was not, as apologists for the bailouts claim, the only hope for GM and Chrysler. And the long-term costs of the bailouts will be enormous.

In late 2008, then-Treasury Secretary Henry Paulson tapped the $700 billion Troubled Asset Relief Fund to lend more than $17 billion to General Motors and Chrysler. With the fate of the car companies still uncertain at the outset of the Obama administration in 2009, Mr. Obama set up an auto task force headed by "car czar" Steve Rattner.

Under the strategy that was chosen, each of the companies was required to file for bankruptcy as a condition of receiving additional funding. Rather than undergo a restructuring under ordinary bankruptcy rules, however, each corporation pretended to "sell" its assets to a new entity that was set up for the purposes of the sale.

With Chrysler, the new entity paid $2 billion, which went to Chrysler's senior lenders, giving them a small portion of the $6.9 billion they were owed. (Fiat was given a large stake in the new entity, although it did not contribute any money). But the "sale" also ensured that Chrysler's unionized retirees would receive a big recovery on their $10 billion claim—a $4.6 billion promissory note and 55% of Chrysler's stock—even though they were lower priority creditors.

A Sham Sale

If other bidders were given a legitimate opportunity to top the $2 billion of government money on offer, this might have been a legitimate transaction. But they weren't. A bid wouldn't count as "qualified" unless it had the same strings as the government bid—a sizeable payment to union retirees and full payment of trade debt. If a bidder wanted to offer $2.5 billion for Chrysler's Jeep division, he was out of luck. With General Motors, senior creditors didn't get trampled in the same way. But the "sale," which left the government with 61% of GM's stock, was even more of a sham.

If the government wanted to "sell" the companies in bankruptcy, it should have held real auctions and invited anyone to bid. But the government decided that there was no need to let pesky rule-of-law considerations interfere with its plan to help out the unions and other favored creditors. Victims of defective GM and Chrysler cars waiting to be paid damages weren't so fortunate—they'll end up getting nothing or next to nothing.

Nor would both companies simply have collapsed if the government hadn't orchestrated the two transactions. General Motors was a perfectly viable company that could have been restructured under the ordinary reorganization process. The only serious question was GM's ability to obtain financing for its bankruptcy, given the credit market conditions in 2008. But even if financing were not available—and there's a very good chance it would have been—the government could have provided funds without also usurping the bankruptcy process.

Although Chrysler wasn't nearly so healthy, its best divisions—Jeep in particular—would have survived in a normal bankruptcy, either through restructuring or through a sale to a more viable company. This is very similar to what the government bailout did, given that Chrysler is essentially being turned over to Fiat.

The Indirect Costs

The claim that the bailouts were done at little cost is even more dubious. This side of the story rests on the observation that GM's success in selling a significant amount of stock, reducing the government's stake, and Chrysler's repayment of its loans, show that the direct costs to taxpayers may be lower than many originally feared. But this doesn't mean that taxpayers are off the hook. They are still likely to end up with a multibillion dollar bill—nearly $14 billion, according to current White House estimates.

But the $14 billion figure omits the cost of the previously accumulated tax losses GM can apply against future profits, thanks to a special post-bailout government gift. The ordinary rule is that these losses can only be preserved after bankruptcy if the company is restructured—not if it's sold. By waiving this rule, the government saved GM at least $12 billion to $13 billion in future taxes, a large chunk of which (not all, because taxpayers also own GM stock) came straight out of taxpayers' pockets.

To claim that the car companies would have collapsed if the government hadn't intervened in the way it did, and to suggest that the intervention came at very little cost, is a dangerous misreading of our recent history.

The indirect costs may be the worst problem here. The car bailouts have sent the message that, if a politically important industry is in trouble, the government may step in, rearrange the existing creditors' normal priorities, and dictate the result it wants. Lenders will be very hesitant to extend credit under these conditions.

This will make it much harder, and much more costly, for a company in a politically sensitive industry to borrow money when it is in trouble. As a result, the government will face even more pressure to step in with a bailout in the future. In effect, the government is crowding out the ordinary credit markets.

None of this suggests that we should be unhappy with the recent success of General Motors and Chrysler. Their revival is a very encouraging development. But to claim that the car companies would have collapsed if the government hadn't intervened in the way it did, and to suggest that the intervention came at very little cost, is a dangerous misreading of our recent history.

15

Government-Sponsored Mortgage Enterprise Bailouts Benefit Homeowners

Daniel Gross

Daniel Gross, a Yahoo Finance *columnist, is the author of* Dumb Money: How Our Greatest Financial Minds Bankrupted the Nation.

The costs of the bailout of Fannie Mae and Freddie Mac, government-sponsored mortgage firms designed to promote homeownership, will be offset by the benefits to American taxpayers. The implied government guarantee allows Fannie Mae and Freddie Mac to borrow at much lower rates, which it passes on to American borrowers. These low-interest home loans collectively save American borrowers billions. Moreover, unlike some of the large investment banks, Fannie Mae and Freddie Mac did not make many high-risk loans. While the cost of the bailout of Fannie and Freddie may indeed be high, the benefit to home owning taxpayers is greater.

On Sunday [July 13, 2008], Washington policymakers announced details of a plan to shore up Fannie Mae [the Federal National Mortgage Association] and Freddie Mac [the Federal Home Loan Mortgage Corporation], the struggling government-sponsored enterprises [GSEs] that are huge players in the mortgage market. The proposals—a plan for both the Treasury Department and the Federal Reserve to extend credit to the listing giants, if needed, and a proposal for Congress to give Treasury the authority to buy shares in the companies, if needed—were immediately characterized as a bailout.

The bailout will be a bargain for American taxpayers, because any cost of it will be overwhelming offset by the tangible and quantifiable economic benefits that taxpayers have collectively received over the years.

But the actions don't amount to a bailout—yet. The announcements simply constituted the final explicit declaration of what investors, politicians, and policymakers around the world have long taken as an implicit assumption: that the U.S. government would back the debt of Fannie Mae and Freddie Mac. Questions have been raised about the potential cost to taxpayers if the government ultimately does have to help the two companies make good on the debt they've sold to investors. But as it turns out, under almost any circumstances, the bailout will be a bargain for American taxpayers, because any cost of it will be overwhelmingly offset by the tangible and quantifiable economic benefits that taxpayers have collectively received over the years from the market's expectations that such a bailout would materialize if needed.

Passing the Savings on to Borrowers

Fannie Mae and Freddie Mac occupy a strange netherworld between the U.S. government (whose debt can never fail) and the corporate world (where debt occasionally fails). Fannie and Freddie borrow money in the public markets at rates somewhere between what the government pays and what a good corporate borrower would. Over the years, economists have attempted to quantify the government-sponsored enterprise's advantage—and how much of that advantage it passes on to borrowers in the form of lower costs. On its Web site, Freddie Mac quotes the Office of Management Budget thus: "[M]ortgage rates are 25–50 basis points lower because Fannie Mae and Freddie Mac exist in the form and size they do." (Twenty-five to 50 basis points is one-quarter to one-half a point, in layman's terms.) Freddie goes on to say that "because the secondary mortgage market saves homebuyers up to one half percent on their mortgage, borrowers nationwide save an average of nearly $23.5 billion annually." That may be overstating the case. Economist Lawrence J. White of New York University's Stern School of Business says the consensus among economists holds that the implied guarantee allows Fannie and Freddie to borrow at rates between 35 and 40 basis points lower than rates available to analogous companies that don't have an implicit government backing. If Bank X pays 5.35 percent to borrow, Fannie Mae pays only 5. The government-sponsored enterprises pass on most—but not all—of those savings to consumers in the form of lower interest rates on mortgages. Again, White says the consensus is about 25 basis points.

But 25 basis points—one-quarter of one percentage point—can add up to significant savings on large amounts of money. At the end of 2007, Fannie and Freddie held or guaranteed mortgages worth about $5.2 trillion. . . . This means that borrowers saved about $13 billion in 2007 on interest costs, thanks to the GSEs. The numbers were lower in previous years. Assuming a 25-basis-point savings, the savings were $7.5 billion in 2001 and $3.25 billion in 1994. Calculating the cumulative present-day value of the historic implied guarantee—after all, $3.25 billion in 1994 is worth about $4.75 billion in today's dollars—would be a complicated task. But after laying out all sorts of caveats, Lawrence White believes it could add up to more than $100 billion in current dollars.

Helping Homeowners

So, merely by signaling to the markets that it might back the GSEs' debt, the government has, over the past few decades, helped tens of millions of homeowners save some serious money. Until this week, the cost of this benefit has been effectively nothing—save for some foregone taxes and the cost of regulating the companies. But if Fannie and Freddie exhaust the patience of the private sector—the shareholders—and can't raise capital to make up for losses on the mortgage portfolio—they would have to turn to the government. How much would they need?

Big hypothetical costs for taxpayers . . . would still be smaller than the actual benefits taxpayers—or at least the large majority of taxpayers who are homeowners— have already received.

This is a great unknown. But it's hard to imagine it would approach a figure close to $100 billion. Fannie Mae and Freddie Mac didn't make subprime loans, although they do have some exposure to subprime debt through assets they purchased. Rather, they make loans to people who make down payments and who buy houses under a certain price (the maximum loan last year was $417,000). As a result, the companies avoided funding lots of mortgages in expensive, bubbly markets. In the fourth quarter of 2007, the delinquency rates for mortgages on single-family homes were 0.65 percent for Freddie Mac and 0.98 percent for Fannie Mae.

Let's assume for the moment that 5 percent of the $5.2 trillion in mortgages that Fannie Mae and Freddie Mac hold or insure goes bad, which would represent a massive (and unlikely) uptick from current numbers. Lawrence White says that because of the company's underwriting standards, the losses on those loans would be only about 30 percent. Run the numbers, and the potential losses—i.e., the amount of federal funds needed to make bond investors whole assuming the GSEs can't raise any more outside capital—would be about $78 billion. If 2 percent of the mortgages the GSEs hold or insure goes bad—a much more reasonable guess—the government would have to come up with about $31 billion. Those are big hypothetical costs for taxpayers. But they would still be smaller than the actual benefits taxpayers—or at least the large majority of taxpayers who are homeowners—have already received.

16

Government-Sponsored Mortgage Enterprise Bailouts Penalize Taxpayers

Adam Berkland

Adam Berkland is a legislative assistant at Americans for Prosperity, a grassroots organization that favors limited government and free markets.

The bailout of the government-sponsored mortgage enterprises Fannie Mae and Freddie Mac puts taxpayer money at risk. Replacing the implicit government guarantee of these mortgage companies with an explicit one does not change the fact that the government should not be in the mortgage business. Government management is subject to political influences. In fact, the desire to keep mortgage rates low led Congress to relax the standards that kept Fannie and Freddie afloat. When the housing bubble collapsed, Fannie and Freddie began to fail. The decision to bail them out forces taxpayers to pay for poor congressional decisions and the risks taken by private investors.

With a $154 billion bailout of Fannie Mae [the Federal National Mortgage Association] and Freddie Mac [the Federal Home Loan Mortgage Corporation] thus far, and regulators estimating the need for billions more, lawmakers in Washington have finally begun debate on how to wind down these two failed mortgage giants. While there is widespread agreement that they must be eliminated gradually to avoid market disruptions, plans for what will replace Fannie and Freddie have not found similar consensus.

A Questionable Plan

One plan has recently gained attention on Capitol Hill, not the least because it has emerged from a surprising source. In early May [2011] the typically small-government conservative Rep. John Campbell (R.-Calif.) teamed up with Rep. Gary Peters (D.-Mich.) to introduce the Housing Finance Reform Act, HR 1859, mirroring an Obama administration proposal released earlier this year. Campbell apparently believes that Fannie and Freddie simply provided the *wrong kind* of government support for the housing market, not that government support itself was the problem. Campbell's mind-set is reminiscent of Friedrich Hayek's book on the failure of socialism *The Fatal Conceit.* If we could just get the *right kind* of government support in place, we could continue to subsidize low mortgage rates and the 30-year fixed-rate mortgage while simultaneously protecting taxpayers from the risk of future bailouts.

This time, it will be different, he says. This time the government's guarantee to mortgage investors would be explicit, and significant layers of private capital would stand as a butter before taxpayer funds are used to prop up the market. Should losses occur on soured mortgages, taxpayers would chip in only after homeowners' equity and the security issuers' shareholders are completely wiped out and a special Federal Deposit Insurance Corporation (FDIC)-like reserve fund is entirely depleted. By building strong buffers and with careful regulation, taxpayers are sure to be safe, right?

Don't be fooled. Campbell's plan strays far from limited-government principles, simply replacing the failed Fannie Mae and Freddie Mac model with another form of government support, once again putting taxpayer dollars at risk to subsidize mortgages and protect investors from mortgage-related losses. Joining a growing chorus of critics, American Enterprise Institute scholar Alex Pollock explained the flaw in this plan at a recent hearing:

> "Remember that this theory of having private capital in front of government risk was exactly the theory of Fannie Mae and Freddie Mac, and in the 1990s, when their risk-based capital was set up, the theory was that this risk-based capital would allow them to survive a new Depression. Obviously it was all wrong."

The Political Pressures

We've seen in the past that when government is running the show, prudential management typically gives way to political pressures. In the years leading up to the financial crisis, Congress relaxed or simply didn't enforce Fannie's and Freddie's capital standards, leaving the GSEs (government-sponsored-enterprises) more highly leveraged than their private market competitors. They then blew through their razor-thin capital buffers at an alarming pace as the housing bubble collapsed, with the disastrous results that we've seen today ($154 billion in bailouts and counting. . .).

Reserve funds have also proved to be an unreliable tool, because they tend to be either raided by Congress for other big-government spending projects (as the Social Security Trust Fund has been) or poorly managed (as the recent experience with the FDIC's Deposit Insurance Fund shows). Congress also has strong incentives to reduce the government's "guarantee fees" in order to hold down mortgage rates, thereby underpricing risk in government-backed mortgage investments and underfunding the reserve fund presumably in place to protect taxpayers.

In short, as long as Congress has an interest in keeping mortgage rates low for the homeowners in their districts, they will not be able to resist the temptation to undermine taxpayer protection in the name of affordable housing.

It doesn't matter how many walls you put up if taxpayers, instead of securities investors, are the ones having their pockets raided at the end of the day.

A Moral Hazard

But even if Campbell is right, and all of these protections work precisely as he predicts, he has still forgotten the most important point. If the guarantee associations (first), the reserve fund (second) and taxpayers (third) pick up the tab for any credit losses, when do the *investors in the securities*, those who ultimately fund mortgage loans and stand to profit from them, ever have to face losses? And if investors can't lose, what incentive do they have to choose their mortgage investments carefully? With no market discipline imposed by the prospect of facing real losses, moral hazard would run rampant. The result would be severely underpriced risk (more risky loans), overinvestment in housing (another housing bubble), and a misallocation of capital (diverting funds from other, more productive sectors of the economy).

Campbell has tried to build a regular Fort Knox to protect taxpayers from losses, but even these protections are likely to fail. The reason is that it doesn't matter how many walls you put up if taxpayers, instead of securities investors, are the ones having their pockets raided at the end of the day. Until private investors are the ones bearing the losses on any shoddy investments they make, the very same problems that spurred the recent financial crisis will remain locked in place, and taxpayers will remain on the hook for bailouts running into the billions of dollars.

Organizations to Contact

The editors have compiled the following list of organizations concerned with the issues debated in this book. The descriptions are derived from materials provided by the organizations. All have publications or information available for interested readers. The list was compiled on the date of publication of the present volume; the information provided here may change. Be aware that many organizations take several weeks or longer to respond to inquiries, so allow as much time as possible.

American Enterprise Institute (AEI)
1150 17th St. NW, Washington, DC   20036
(202) 862-5800 • fax: (202) 862-7177
website: www.aei.org

AEI is a nonpartisan, public policy institute dedicated to promoting the value of limited government, private industry, personal responsibility, and government accountability. The organization generally espouses a belief in the ability of free markets to overcome economic downturn and instability; however, in the wake of the recent financial crisis, AEI scholars have supported nationalizing certain economic cornerstones, such as American banks, in an effort to stabilize the economy. Articles examining the pros and cons of federal involvement in private industry can be read in AEI's monthly publication the *American*, with additional articles, commentary, and testimony available on the AEI website, including "Were the 2008 Bailouts Justified?" and "Taking on the Notion of 'Too Big to Fail.'"

The Brookings Institution
1775 Massachusetts Ave. NW, Washington, DC   20036
(202) 797-6000 • fax: (202) 797-6004
e-mail: brookinfo@brook.edu
website: www.brookings.edu

The institution is devoted to nonpartisan research, education, and publication in economics, government, foreign policy, and the social sciences. Its principal purposes are to aid in the development of sound public policies and to promote public understanding of issues of national importance. While Brookings generally supports the bailout to prevent economic collapse, it urges caution and supports regulatory reform. It publishes the quarterly journals the *Brookings Review* and *Brookings Papers on Economic Activity.* On its website Brookings publishes opinions, interviews, and videos on the bailouts, including "More Nuance Needed in Bank Regulations" and "Wall Street, Main Street, and Wages After the Bailouts."

Cato Institute

1000 Massachusetts Ave. NW, Washington, DC   20001
(202) 842-0200 • fax: (202) 842-3490
website: www.cato.org

A libertarian public policy think-tank, Cato advocates limited government involvement in both the economic and social lives of American citizens and companies. As to the government's decision to bail out private industry in light of the ongoing financial crisis, Cato cautions against extensive government involvement, warning that when the government intervenes in the matters of private industry, the potential exists for unconstitutional imposition of restrictions on individuals and corporations. Cato publications include the quarterly magazine *Regulation* and the bimonthly newsletter *Cato Policy Report.* Articles and testimony by CATO analysts can be accessed at Cato's website, including "Is the Bailout Constitutional?" and "Lasting Implications of the General Motors Bailout."

Center for American Progress (CAP)

1333 H St. NW, 10th Floor, Washington, DC   20005
(202) 682-1611 • fax: (202) 682-1867
e-mail: progress@americanprogress.org
website: www.americanprogress.org

CAP was founded in 2003 to advance a progressive alternative to conservative ideas present in American politics. The center promotes public policy that it believes restores America's position as a global leader, focuses on the creation and use of clean energy technology, provides economic opportunity for all, and offers universal health care to all Americans. CAP believes the bailout of private industry to be a necessary step in reestablishing the stability of the American economy and promoting future growth. Analysis of the financial crisis can be found on the organization's website, including the article "Don't Roll Back Wall Street Reform" and the report, *A Responsible Market for Housing Finance.*

Center for Economic and Policy Research (CEPR)

1611 Connecticut Avenue NW, Suite 400
Washington, DC   20009
(202) 293-5380 • fax: (202)588-1356
e-mail: cepr@cepr.net
website: www.cepr.net

CEPR was co-founded by economists Dean Baker and Mark Weisbrot in 1999 to promote democratic debate on important economic and social issues. Believing that an informed public should be able to choose policies that improve quality of life, both for people within the United States and around the world, the center conducts professional research and public education oriented towards filling important gaps in the understanding of particular economic and social problems, or the impact of specific policies. Some CEPR experts claim that while the bailout may have saved Wall Street, it failed to protect homeowners or put an end to risky practices. The center publishes articles, editorials, reports, and testimony concerning the financial crisis and the bailouts on its website, including "The Failures of TARP" and "Full Cost-Benefit Analysis of AIG Bailout."

Economic Policy Institute (EPI)

1333 H St. NW, Suite 300, East Tower
Washington, DC   20005
(202) 775-8810 • fax: (202) 775-0819

e-mail: epi@epi.org
website: www.epi.org

EPI, a non-profit Washington, DC think-tank, seeks to ensure that the interests of low- and middle-income workers are represented and considered in the national debate about economic policy. The institute views the government bailout of private industry as essential to ensuring the stability of the American economy and the continued employment of many low- and middle-income workers who would be among the first to lose their jobs should certain industries declare bankruptcy. Additionally, EPI favors a financial industry bailout plan with conditions that protect the taxpayers, whose money will be used to fund the plan, from significant losses. EPI publications and reports can be read online, including commentary such as "Bailouts Helping Big Banks Get Bigger" and the report *Rebuilding the Framework for Financial Regulation.*

Federal Reserve
20th St. and Constitution Ave. NW, Washington, DC   20551
website: www.federalreserve.gov

Established on December 23, 1913, the Federal Reserve, or the Fed, is the central bank of the United States. The Fed influences money and credit conditions, oversees banking institutions and regulates their activity, aids in the maintenance of economic stability by containing risk, and provides financial services to the US government and public. Members of the Federal Reserve board have provided testimony and speeches concerning the current financial crisis and bailout measures, transcripts of which are available on its website.

Foundation for Economic Education (FEE)
30 S. Broadway, Irvington-on-Hudson, NY   10533
(914) 591-7230 • fax: (914) 591-8910
website: www.fee.org

FEE is an organization, founded in 1946, to promote the principles of free-market economics and the "freedom philosophy." FEE has criticized the different bailout packages that have provided government aid to struggling private companies throughout the current recession, maintaining that free market economics, not government intervention, will provide the stimulus the economy needs to rebound and stabilize. The foundation publishes the monthly *Freeman*, recent articles from which are available on its website, including "The Financial Bailouts: 'See the Needle and the Damage Done.'"

Heritage Foundation
214 Massachusetts Ave. NE, Washington, DC   20002
(202) 546-4400 • fax: (202) 546-8328
e-mail: info@heritage.org
website: www.heritage.org

Heritage is a conservative public policy research institute that seeks to advance national government policies developed using the ideas of free market economics, limited government involvement in private industry, individual freedom, and a strong national defense. The organization opposes the use of federal money to bail out private industry, maintaining that government spending neither stimulates economic growth nor encourages fledgling private companies to improve their business models. Commentary, reports, and audio on the bailouts can be found on the foundation's website, including "Auto Money Mischief" and "TARP II: How It Will Affect You and Your Tax Dollars."

National Bureau of Economic Research (NBER)
1050 Massachusetts Ave., Cambridge, MA   02138
(617) 868-3900 • fax: (617) 868-2742
e-mail: info@nber.org
website: http://nber.org

Since its founding in 1920, NBER has been working to provide unbiased, accurate information about the state of the national and global economy to policymakers, professionals, and academics. During the current global economic crisis, NBER publishes and disseminates reports that provide explanations of how the situation occurred and what options exist to solve current problems. Publications of the organization include the monthly *NBER Digest* and the quarterly *NBER Reporter*. Copies of these publications as well as other articles and reports can be accessed online.

Reason Foundation
3415 S. Sepulveda Blvd., Suite 400, Los Angeles, CA   90034
(310) 391-2245 • fax: (310) 391-4395
website: http://reason.org

Reason Foundation was founded in 1968 to encourage the development and implementation of policies based on the Libertarian principles of free market economics, individual liberty, and the rule of law. As such, Reason has generally opposed the recent bailouts of private industry, arguing that competition and innovation coupled with a free market economy are the best solution to the current economic crisis, not increased government spending that rewards failing industries. Articles on the bailouts can be found in Reason *Magazine*, the monthly publication of the organization. Comprehensive coverage of the ongoing recession and proposed bailout and stimulus bills can also be found on the foundation's website.

United States Government Accountability Office (GAO)
414 G St. NW, Washington, DC   20548
(202) 512-3000
e-mail: contact@gao.gov
website: www.gao.gov

As the investigative arm of the US government, the GAO serves as a watchdog, ensuring that government policies benefit the American people. Currently, the GAO has published numerous reports outlining the causes of the current recession and analyzing policies being developed and implemented to combat the economic crisis. Copies of these reports can be accessed at the GAO website.

Bibliography

Books

Marc Jarsulic   *Anatomy of a Financial Crisis: A Real Estate Bubble, Runaway Credit Markets, and Regulatory Failure.* New York: Palgrave Macmillan, 2010.

Robert W. Kolb   *The Financial Crisis of Our Time.* New York: Oxford University Press, 2011.

Robert W. Kolb, ed.   *Lessons from the Financial Crisis: Causes, Consequences, and Our Economic Future.* Hoboken, NJ: Wiley, 2010.

Roger Lowenstein   *The End of Wall Street.* New York: Penguin, 2010.

Lawrence G. McDonald and Patrick Robinson   *A Colossal Failure of Common Sense: The Inside Story of the Collapse of Lehman Brothers.* New York: Crown Business, 2009.

Adam Michaelson   *The Foreclosure of America: The Inside Story of the Rise and Fall of Countrywide Home Loans, the Mortgage Crisis, and the Default of the American Dream.* New York: Berkley Books, 2009.

Charles R. Morris   *The Trillion Dollar Meltdown.* New York: Public Affairs, 2008.

Paul Muolo

$700 Billion Bailout: The Emergency Economic Stabilization Act and What It Means to You, Your Money, Your Mortgage, and Your Taxes. Hoboken, NJ: Wiley, 2009.

Tomson H. Nguyen

Fraud and the Subprime Mortgage Crisis. El Paso, TX: LFB Scholarly, 2011.

Kevin Phillips

Bad Money: Reckless Finance, Failed Politics, and the Global Crisis of American Capitalism. New York: Viking, 2008.

Nicolas P. Retsinas and Eric S. Belsky, eds.

Moving Forward: The Future of Consumer Credit and Mortgage Finance. Washington, DC: Brookings Institution Press, 2011.

Barry Ritholtz

Bailout Nation: How Greed and Easy Money Corrupted Wall Street and Shook the World Economy. Hoboken, NJ: John Wiley & Sons, 2009.

Thomas A. Russo and Aaron J. Katzel

The 2008 Financial Crisis and Its Aftermath: Addressing the Next Debt Challenge. Washington, DC: Group of Thirty, 2011.

Andre Ross Sorkin

Too Big to Fail: The Inside Story of How Wall Street and Washington Fought to Save the Financial System—and Themselves. New York: Penguin, 2010.

Robert E. Wright   *Bailouts: Public Money, Private Profit.*
New York: Columbia University
Press, 2010.

Periodicals and Internet Sources

Fred Barnes   "The Other American Auto
Industry," *Weekly Standard*, December
22, 2008.

Ken Bensinger   "Masses Aren't Buying Bailout," *Los
Angeles Times*, September 26, 2008.

Thomas J.   "Auto Industry's Future," *CQ*
Billitteri   *Researcher*, February 6, 2009.

Thomas J.   "Financial Bailout," *CQ Researcher*,
Billitteri   October 24, 2008.

Alex Blumenthal   "Too Big to Succeed," Govexec.com,
December 28, 2011.

Jay Bookman   "Putting Politicians in Charge of
Detroit?" *Atlanta
Journal/Constitution*, December 8,
2008.

Gail Russell   "A Government-run Auto Industry?"
Chaddock   *Christian Science Monitor*, December
10, 2008.

Jamie Choi and   "Leveling the Playing Field: Dr.
Jim Wallis   Elizabeth Warrant—Head of
Congress's TARP Watchdog and
Veteran Sunday School
Teacher—Talks with Sojourners
About Facing Down the Goliaths of
Wall Street," *Sojourners*, April 2010.

Julie Creswell   "Protected by Washington, Companies Ballooned," *New York Times*, July 13, 2008.

Ken Dilanian   "How Congress Set the State for a Fiscal Meltdown," *USA Today*, October 13, 2008.

Charles Duhigg   "At Freddie Mac, Chief Discarded Warning Signs," *New York Times*, August 5, 2008.

Peter Foster   "Auto Bailouts in One Lesson," *Financial Post*, May 31, 2011.

Ryan Grim   "Lawmakers Regret Deregulating," *Politico*, September 25, 2008.

John Heilemann   "The Wall Street Mind: Triumphant ... To the Victors Belong the Spoils, Right?" *New York*, April 18, 2011.

Michael Hudson   "Why the Bail Out of Freddie Mac and Fanny Mae Is Bad Economic Policy," counterpunch.org, July 15, 2008.

Daniel K. Ikenson   "Bailouts Beget More Bailouts," *USA Today*, June 16, 2011.

William F. Jasper   "From 'Henny Penny' Morgenthau to Henry Paulson: $700 Billion Bailout Are Eerily Similar to Those of FDR's New Deal, and Today's Pied Pipers Are Playing the Same Bipartisan, Power-grabbing Tune," *New American*, November 10, 2008.

Garrett Johnson — "The Biggest Financial Bailout of Them All," *Huffington Post*, March 6, 2010.

Floyd Norris — "How Voters See the Bailout," *New York Times*, October 18, 2008.

Steven Rattner and Scott Cendrowski — "The Auto Bailout: How We Did It," *Fortune*, November 9, 2009.

Ron Scherer — "Fannie Mae and Freddie Mac 101: How Much Will We Miss Them?" *Christian Science Monitor*, February 11, 2011.

Allan Sloan and Doris Burke — "Surprise! The Big Bad Bailout Is Paying Off," *Fortune*, July 25, 2011.

Roy C. Smith — "The Dilemma of Bailouts," *Independent Review*, Summer 2011.

Kevin D. Williamson — "Blame Milton Friedman: Or, How I Learned to Stop Worrying and Love the Bailout," *National Review*, September 21, 2009.

Kevin D. Williamson — "Shadow Bailouts: The Democrats Punish Wall Street with Promises of Endless Money," *National Review*, May 17, 2010.

Andy Zelleke — "Beyond a Bailout, Wall Street Needs New Rules," *Christian Science Monitor*, September 23, 2008.

Sam Zuckerman — "The Dawn of Wall Street 2.0," *San Francisco Chronicle*, October 5, 2008.

Todd Zywicki   "The Auto Bailout and the Rule of
                   Law," *National Affairs*, Spring 2011.

Index